the Butterfly Girl

Racheal Baughan
Foreword by Trisha Goddard

the
Butterfly
Girl

JOHN BLAKE

Published by John Blake Publishing Ltd,
3 Bramber Court, 2 Bramber Road,
London W14 9PB, England

www.blake.co.uk

First published in hardback in 2008

ISBN: 978-1-84454-548-3

British Library Cataloguing-in-Publication Data:

A catalogue record for this book is available from the British Library.

Design by www.envydesign.co.uk

Printed in Great Britain by William Clowes Ltd, Beccles, Suffolk

1 3 5 7 9 10 8 6 4 2

Papers used by John Blake Publishing are natural, recyclable products made
from wood grown in sustainable forests. The manufacturing processes
conform to the environmental regulations of the country of origin.

'It is easy to get bored of what you have when you see it in the mirror every day, but remember, to everyone else you are unique.'

James Baughan

This book is dedicated to the memory of my
best friend, Fay Greene.

Make the most of every day of your life and live it to
the full, as you never know when it will all be over.

Acknowledgements

The unwavering love and support of my family have helped me get through some very difficult and miserable times, and I want to thank my mother and father, Jenny and Anthony, my brothers, James, Geoff, Jason and Andrew, and my sister, Jennifer. I'm also grateful to my niece Lia for making me realise that we need healthier role models within the modelling industry.

Despite what we've been through, Paul Morris deserves my gratitude for helping me take my first steps towards recovery by encouraging me to believe in myself.

I am grateful also to Trisha Goddard for her continued support and for always believing in me, and to the media and my publisher, John Blake, for giving me the opportunity to speak out about BDD and help create some much-needed awareness.

Thank you to all my friends for standing by me, and to Jane Smith for helping me close the past chapters of my life and move on with my future.

Perhaps most importantly, thank you to Fay Greene for making me realise just how precious life is.

Contents

Foreword
by Trisha Goddard

The first time I met Racheal Baughan, she was a guest on my daytime chat show *Trisha*. Her despairing mother literally dragged her along, desperate for help. How do you understand such a pretty daughter who, on one hand, seemed to despise the way she looked and, on the other, was obsessed with her looks? Having spent some twenty years working with people with mental health problems, I quickly realised that praise and platitudes would be a waste of time and just listening to Racheal with my heart and my soul would be the best gift I could give. I knew there would never be a quick fix. I also knew from meeting Racheal on that first show that, without knowing it at the time, deep down she actually had the courage and the wherewithal to do her own fixing – in her own time. Thus, over the years, I asked the producers to keep in touch with her and invite her back on the show.

In the early days she hid under a hat and behind her hair. Recently, Racheal was yet again a guest on my Channel Five show – but this time as an expert to give advice to another guest going through similar turmoil as she once had. I sincerely hope she was proud of herself, because I, sure as hell, was proud of her!

Racheal has truly been there, done it – been all the way back there again, struggled to do it all again and then some – but finally and deservedly got the T-shirt! Her story and her journey opened the eyes of viewers with a negative stereotype of what it means to have a mental illness like BDD and have encouraged others who thought there was no way out of their hell to realise that the first step is to own up to a problem, get help and, step-by-step, walk into wellness.

The great thing about *The Butterfly Girl* is that it's about *living* with a mental health problem; after all, Racheal's been on a fair few television shows, she's been a beauty queen, attracted tabloid newspaper attention thanks to a grubby pop star, as well as having had numerous other articles written about her struggles with BDD. Every great explorer keeps a journal on his or her travels into new territories and *The Butterfly Girl* is Racheal's journal of the type of struggle an estimated 1 in 4 of us will have with mental ill-health.

Racheal is a butterfly still discovering the power of her wings; on some days she can soar and on others a bitter wind may suddenly spring up and temporarily blow her off course. But, whatever happens, now she knows what it feels like to have strength in those brightly-coloured wings, Rachel will never forget that, whatever help she may (or may not) have received, ultimately she taught herself how to fly.

Always did believe in the girl ...

Trisha Goddard

1

My Family and Other Animals

Standing behind the curtain, I feel sick with anxiety. My palms are sweating and the sound of my rapidly beating heart is echoing loudly in my ears as I fight the sudden overwhelming desire to run. I look around me and see 35 beautiful girls, and my panic increases as I desperately try to think why I'm here. Then, as I force myself to take a slow, deep breath, I remember: I am here to prove to the world that the best way to overcome your greatest fears is to face them.

It is 2004 and if anyone had told me two years ago that I would be a contender in the Miss England finals, I would have thought there was more chance of my growing wings and flying. But then that is, in a way, what I am doing. Like a bird leaving its nest for the first time, I am flying on the wings of my newfound independence.

Above the sound of my racing heart I hear the soft music that is the cue for us to start walking out on to the stage, and I begin to repeat my mantra silently in my head: 'Lights! Camera! Action! Chin up, shoulders back, small footsteps.' As I step out on to the red carpet, I hold my head up high and remember what my brother told me: 'Be yourself, keep smiling and show confidence. Believe in yourself and others will too.'

I am wearing an elegant, cream-coloured evening gown that I designed myself. The light chiffon that covers its silk lining trails off into flowing petals as it brushes along the floor. I am proud of how amazing it looks and, for the first time in my life, I feel like a beautiful princess, not because of what I see in the mirror, but because I am experiencing a sensation I can never remember having had before – pride, pride in the bravery I have shown by facing the world. Like Cinderella, I am walking away from the ugly sisters – only the 'ugly sisters' in my case are the voices that have reverberated in my head for so many years.

As my name is announced, I hear cheers from the crowd and catch a glimpse of my family through the blinding glare of the lights on the catwalk. My mother is beaming with pride; my brother James and his wife Caroline are giving me the thumbs-up; and I can see tears of joy in the eyes of my boyfriend Paul and my friend Belinda. Seeing the happiness on the faces of these people who are so important to me, and who have witnessed my suffering over the past few years and played such a huge part in my journey to recovery, I am filled with a feeling of overwhelming satisfaction and immense achievement.

For them, and for me, this day marks the end of a nightmare.

A happy but painfully shy little girl, I was comfortable only with the members of my own extended and close family. Doted on by my three older brothers, Geoff, Jason and James, I was also close to my half-sister Jennifer and half-brother Andrew from my dad's previous marriage.

My brothers meant the world to me as I was growing up, and I'd follow them everywhere. Geoff, who was 11 when I was born, was like a dad to me, and Jason, who's ten years older than me, would spend endless amounts of time teaching me how to draw, taking photos of me and watching me mimic him styling his perfect hair in the mirror. James is the nearest to my age, at just six years older. He was my idol as a child and I'd follow him around endlessly, copying everything he did. Adventurous and a risk taker, he was convinced he was Superman and was always jumping off things, the higher the better. His favourite occupation was leaping from a third-floor window of our house, which, miraculously, never resulted in his receiving any serious injuries. But one day my dad happened to come into the room just as I was balanced precariously on the windowsill ready to copy James's latest death-defying leap – and our jumping days were over.

Some of my happiest childhood memories were of sitting around the dining table with all the family, eating the really good roast dinners my mum used to cook. I was a child with a very large appetite, so there'd always be a fight for the food, with my brothers shouting, 'Quick! Get some food before Racheal eats it all!'

Jennifer lived with her mother, but Andrew came to live with my mum and dad soon after his parents split up, when he was about 11. Four years later, on the day that I was born, he'd just cycled the ten miles to school when he received a call to say Mum had gone into labour, and promptly turned around and cycled 15 miles to the hospital. He was delighted to have a new baby sister and throughout my childhood we were very close. He'd carry me everywhere with him on his hip; in fact, it was Andrew who managed to wean me off my bottle when I was about two years old. I remember being in my cot saying, 'Bot bot,' and Andrew explaining to me that while I was sleeping the birdies came and took it away. Enchanted by the vision of white doves coming into my room and wrapping up the bottle before flying off with it up into the sky, I drank happily from a beaker from then on.

Jennifer was 13 when I was born and, although she didn't live with us, she was like a big sister to me when I was young, and having her in my life was very special. I'd sometimes go to stay at her house, where I'd play for hours on end with her two white Persian cats, which she referred to as her 'babies'. But perhaps one of the main memories of her when I was young is of the great presents she always brought me. Every Christmas I'd look forward to her arriving, and she'd walk through the door with two bin liners full of exciting things. Jennifer was a perfectionist; for example, her wardrobe was very carefully organised and she'd have a place for everything, with labels for bags and shoes. Looking back, I do wonder if it was a bit of an obsession and whether a degree of obsessive-compulsive disorder might run in my family.

However, very sadly, when I was eight there were some splits in the family that resulted in my not seeing either Andrew or Jennifer for several years. I never really understood what happened with Andrew, as all I remember is being in my bedroom doing colouring one day when I heard screaming. As I ran down the stairs, I could see Andrew and my cousin Stephen at the door, shouting at my dad. Stephen was holding a baseball bat, threatening to smash up Dad's Jaguar, and as I stood there terrified, not knowing what was going on, Andrew suddenly saw me and shouted, 'Get Racheal out of here. I don't want her to see this.' My brother Geoff took me by the hand and said, 'Come on, darling. Let's go upstairs.'

When I was a little girl I'd block out anything distressing and within five minutes I was colouring again, with Geoff by my side teaching me a new technique. I think my family always tried to protect me from 'bad situations' and someone would quickly divert my attention in the hope that I'd soon forget what was going on. It did seem to work at the time, but the fact that these events stick in my mind shows that I was more aware of them than I realised.

Just three or four months after Andrew and my family had stopped talking, Jennifer was due to get married and I was very excited because I was going to be a bridesmaid. One day we were all in the kitchen and my mum, dad and Jennifer were discussing the wedding. Despite the fact that my dad and Jennifer's mum had been separated for more than 20 years, Jennifer was saying that she wanted them to travel to the wedding together in the car, to sit together at the 'top table' and be together in all the wedding photos, as though they were still married. She obviously didn't want my mum to be any part of the wedding, which must have made Mum feel very hurt and left out, particularly as she'd been in Jennifer's life since Jennifer was six months old and had played a part in bringing her up.

I suppose Jennifer just felt it would be nice to pretend that her mum and dad were a couple and that she was part of a happy family on her special day, but unfortunately you can't always have things the way you want them to be without hurting other people.

Mum eventually lost her temper, and what had already become a heated discussion turned into a full-scale argument – I was hastily removed to my bedroom yet again, presumably in the hope that I wouldn't notice what was happening. And that was the last time I saw my sister for many years. I wasn't a bridesmaid at her wedding and I never understood why, as an eight-year-old can't really make any sense of all the complications and hurt feelings that can arise out of that sort of situation.

Having already lost Andrew and Jennifer from my life, there were more upsets to come which, looking back on it now, I realise probably further increased the anxiety and insecurity I already felt as a child.

My cousins Jessica and Raymond and their father, Uncle Ray – Dad's brother – lived with us for a time, and one day, when I was nine, I was in the snooker room of our house messing about with Jessica while my brothers played a game of snooker. We were teasing each other when suddenly Jessica said, 'Jason and Geoffrey are my brothers and not yours,' and stuck out her tongue.

I thought it was a joke, until I saw the reaction of my parents and Uncle Ray and the uncomfortable looks they exchanged. Jessica carried on saying the same thing over and over again, until finally I burst into tears and ran to my mum, begging her to tell me it wasn't true. It was a particularly confusing and upsetting idea to have planted in my mind, as I already felt that all the people I loved were being taken away from me. But, to my relief, Mum just hugged me and said that Jessica was only joking.

Then, a few days later, when Uncle Ray was babysitting me, Jessica started teasing me again, telling me that my mum was lying and that Geoff and Jason weren't my brothers. Angry and upset, I shouted at her, 'Stop saying that. They are. They are.'

Jessica turned to her dad and said, 'Tell her, Dad. Tell her they're my brothers and not hers.'

To my horror, instead of telling her not to be silly, Uncle Ray began to try to explain to me that he and my mother had been married at the age of 16 and had split up when Geoffrey was one and Jason was two, and that Mum and Dad had got together shortly afterwards. Apparently, because my dad and Uncle Ray were very close, and because they thought at the time that it was the best thing to do, Dad had brought Geoff and Jason up as though they were his own sons.

I tried to make sense of what Uncle Ray was telling me, but it was too much for such a young child to take in. I'd grown up believing Jason and Geoffrey were my full brothers, so being told that what I thought I'd known my whole life was untrue made me very distressed, and I was still crying when Mum came home. When I told her what Uncle Ray had said, I think I desperately wanted her to say he was lying, but she confirmed that it was true, explaining it to me again in a way that made a bit more sense to a little girl. 'Daddy and Uncle Ray are brothers, which means they have the same blood anyway, and I'm Jason's and Geoffrey's mummy and your mummy too. So they're still your brothers.'

Although reassured to some extent, I was still very disturbed and kept trying to understand what it all meant, until finally taking some comfort from deciding that they were not my *half*-brothers but rather 80 per cent my brothers.

The incident caused a huge argument between Uncle Ray and my dad, which resulted in Jessica, along with Raymond and Uncle Ray, being taken away from me, because my parents felt it would be best if we all went our separate ways. The wounds inflicted deep inside me by Jessica's revelation will never be completely healed but, although Jason and Geoff are not my 'full' brothers by blood, I still love them and feel as close to them as I did before.

My dad, Tony, is English and a very successful businessman. When I was little he had his own interior-design and double-glazing company, with showrooms across London, and he always worked hard to provide us with the many comforts we enjoyed. However, he has also always been a workaholic by nature and so was seldom home before 10 or 11 at night. One of the highlights of my day as a small child was staying awake until I heard his voice and then rushing downstairs to sit beside him as he ate his dinner. The titbits from his meal that he would put on a plate for me were an added treat, because my mum is an excellent cook. Those evenings were very special to me, as they were the only time I really spent with my dad; if he wasn't out working for his business, he was working at home, decorating or gardening – Dad's never been one to sit still.

My mum, Jenny, is Sri Lankan, a petite and attractive powerhouse of energy who was born into a wealthy family in Sri Lanka. She came to England as a little girl and experienced a very difficult and disturbed childhood before battling her way to a more 'normal' life. The determination and tenacity that helped her then were also to serve me well in the years to come.

With such a large and sociable family, our house was always filled with people, and I spent many childhood hours playing under our big oak dining table, listening to the voices swirling around me and looking at everyone's shoes as they passed by. Too shy to be sociable myself, I determinedly resisted my mum's many attempts to encourage me to make friends with the children who came to the house with their parents, and would cling anxiously to her legs when anyone spoke to me.

My passion in life from a very young age was animals and, thanks to the fact that we lived in a huge old Queen Anne manor house with acres of land, it was one I was free to indulge. From the age of about seven, I bred hamsters, and ended up with 27 of them living on the stack shelves in my room – all of which I insisted on keeping. Well, I say I kept them all, but in fact several of them escaped, some to torment my brothers by giving birth under their beds. It was a joke in the family – and a source of some anxiety for my dad – that the hamsters that escaped would breed with mice and give rise to a whole new species, dozens of which would continue to scurry around the house unseen for years to come.

We also had several dogs, cats and a goat that shared the cats' bed in the kitchen, as well as a donkey, a Shetland pony and a horse, which *did* live outside. I was passionate about horses, and in particular about my own horse, Freckles, and it was my love of horses that led me to make my greatest friend, Fay, at the age of eight.

However, the problem with my love of animals was that I would become so attached to them that their deaths always had a huge psychological effect on me. Because I was never a 'popular' little girl at school, I think I felt that the animals were friends who would never judge me, and each time one of them died I'd feel as though I'd lost a family member and would cry for weeks. Eventually I decided to create a little pets' graveyard in the garden; Dad would bury them and I'd make a cross out of off-cuts of wood and engrave on it the animal's name and the date he or she died. There seemed to be a lot of animals to bury, but I suppose that wasn't surprising when you consider I had more than 50 at one point.

One experience that sticks in my mind is when one of my beloved hamsters had escaped and the whole family was searching for him. I lifted the couch to see if he was underneath it and, seeing no sign of him, dropped it back down again. As I did so, I heard a screech and at the same time noticed that the couch didn't seem to be balanced on the floor properly. So I raised it again, only to find my hamster half-dead under one of its feet. We rushed the hamster to the vet, but it was too late – I had killed him. I hated myself for it and felt very deeply disturbed by what had happened, and the fact that I have tears in my eyes when I think about it now shows just how much the experience upset me.

On another occasion I was devastated when my friend Belinda came running into the house crying and told me that her mother had run over my black Persian cat Bob. Before anyone could stop me I ran outside and saw him lying dead in the road, which is an image that never leaves my mind even now.

Then my puppy was run over by my brother's friend's radio-controlled car and, because he was so small and his injuries were so bad, he had to be put down. My beautiful white kitten was also run over, this time by my mum when she drove off in the car without realising the kitten was asleep on its wheel.

I was spending hours sitting crying in my pets' graveyard, and eventually my dad could see how badly I was being affected by it all. So he told Mum he couldn't bear to see the sadness in my eyes any longer and that I wasn't to have any more animals.

Nowadays, I have a beautiful dog called Peanut. I take her everywhere with me and protect her with my life, as I'm terrified of anything happening to her and having to experience again the pain I went through as a child. Still very much an animal lover, I sometimes dream of giving up my relatively glamorous lifestyle and spending my days working on a farm surrounded by animals – although maybe that's a dream to keep until I retire.

Another factor that may have helped to increase the sense of insecurity I think I've always had was that, when I was about ten, my mum became really ill. She was suffering from severe depression, triggered by specific events in her life, and the doctor put her on Valium. Although she tried to hide it from me, and I certainly didn't understand what was going on at the time, I do remember that there was quite a long period when she never came out of her room. She'd just lie in the dark day after day, in the smallest room of our massive house, and I'd speak to her through the door.

Then one day I was upstairs when I heard an ambulance arriving and, when I went down to the kitchen, Mum was lying on the floor with froth coming out of her mouth. I had no idea what had happened and felt really frightened as I watched her being taken out to the ambulance on a stretcher. I went to visit her in hospital afterwards, but all I can remember is just sitting there crying. She'd taken an overdose and, although I didn't know it at the time, wasn't expected to live.

But eventually she did come out of hospital and was then ill at home for about two years, which was a really difficult time for everyone. I was lucky, because my brother Geoff looked after me and was really good to me. He kept me occupied, made my packed lunches for school, cooked my dinners and took me everywhere. At this stage I was being bullied at school and there were several occasions when we arrived at the school gates and I begged Geoff not to make me go inside. So he'd have to ring

Mum on the phone we had in the car and ask her what to do and, because she was so weak and drained and didn't have the energy to push me, she'd tell him to bring me home. I can't really remember much more about that period, except that Geoff made me really good steak sandwiches and we used to watch the David Bowie film *Labyrinth* together.

However, there is one incident I remember, which I only mention because it illustrates some of the side effects of Valium. We were all down in the kitchen cooking dinner when one of the kids asked Mum something and she suddenly had a fit and threw a pan of hot water across the room. She's a really placid person, so it was even more shocking when she did these erratic, very sudden things because they were completely alien to the way she'd always been before. I realise now that it was due to the Valium, and she eventually had to get help to wean herself off it, which is why she's so adamantly against anti-depressants and why she went on to work at a drugs centre both to try to understand her own experiences and to help people with similar problems. It's because of what happened to Mum that I don't believe anti-depressants fix people's problems; they just put them on hold. But, having said that, I do realise some people need them.

Mum was very ill during that period and I'm sure it's a part of her life she's embarrassed about. But it was probably also a seminal experience for me in some ways: it's obviously not easy to watch that sort of thing happening to your mum. She'd gone from being someone who was always there to being too ill to look after us, and it must have left some kind of impression on me, even though I wasn't aware of it at the time.

2

A Horsey Girl

I've always thought I didn't remember much about my childhood, but I've been surprised by what I've been able to recall since starting to write this book, and by how doing so has helped me to make sense of some things I've never really thought about before.

I was obviously prone to 'identity crises' from a very young age, as at just three years old I decided I no longer wanted to be called Racheal and would say to people, 'Me not Racheal. Me Ed.' This went on until I was at least five, and was apparently something I was very passionate about. So I wonder if even back then I was trying to put on an act and be someone else, and perhaps felt more confident being 'Ed' rather than the painfully shy little girl I really was.

My change of identity was a seemingly random decision that I came to one day after my mum had been watching *Coronation Street* on television. One of the characters was a dustman called Eddie Yates. Why on earth I decided to name myself after him I'll never know; most little girls would like to be Barbie or a princess, but I wanted to be the dustman on *Coronation Street*! Maybe it was my way of rebelling against being thought of as 'pretty'.

My next real recollection is of starting school when I was four and looking round at the other children and thinking I was much older than they were. Being 'different' for one reason or another (none of them good) is a feeling that has stayed with me all my life.

At that stage, having resolutely opposed my mum's attempts to introduce me to other children, I had just one little friend, called Katy Hucker. Our family was well off, so I'd never been short of wonderful, and expensive, presents, but it was Katy who gave me what I thought was the best and most exciting present I'd ever had — a little duck from a Kinder egg, which I used to carry around with me everywhere.

I can remember being very frightened on my first day at school. I was starting in the reception class of a small private school in our village in Surrey, and was desperate at the thought of Mum leaving me alone there; she ended up having to stay throughout the first day to help allay my panic at being surrounded by all the other noisy, apparently confident children. With frequent glances in her direction to reassure myself that she hadn't left, I eventually started playing tentatively with a toy cooker, but my relative serenity was soon shattered when a couple of little boys took some of the pots and pans to make sandcastles. It was enough to shake the very small amount of confidence I had and I apparently indulged in a very loud and tearful strop, accompanied by heartfelt pleas to be taken home.

It was a very strict school and, looking back on it now, it seemed to have some extremely strange and inappropriate rules. But, of course, without any other experience of what a school day involved, I didn't think any of it was odd or worthy of mention at the time. Even at the age of five, we had to do all the washing up after lunch and take turns cleaning the hall floor. The food was horrible, but had to be eaten. On one occasion, when it was particularly revolting and I'd been made to eat every last morsel, I promptly threw it all up again and, as I sat there crying, was told I would also have to eat what I'd regurgitated. It was a step too far, even for a little girl as compliant and 'good' as me, and I refused. But I didn't tell Mum about it until much later, as I had no parameters by which to judge that what the teacher had done was wrong.

The parents' committee was very important and influential in the school and, oddly enough, when it came to sports days – and in fact almost any other competitive event – the children of parents on the committee always managed to win. But on one particular sports day, when I was eight, I won the running race. I was terribly excited, as I'd never previously won anything except an Easter-egg-colouring competition, but my delight was short-lived as it was announced that another little boy called Ben had won. Ben's parents were leading lights of the parents' committee and, despite their protestations that their son had in fact come second, Ben's name was put on the cup and this small, but to me important, victory was snatched away from me.

On another occasion, we had all been told to make a 'secret garden' in a shoebox and, as I was quite artistic, I set about making mine completely unaided and with great enthusiasm. The finished product was brilliant and I was very proud of it. But it proved to be no match for the other elaborate and sophisticated entries in the competition, most of which had been made by the children's parents.

These little disappointments sound petty and insignificant now, but the fact that they have stuck in my memory all these years shows they really mattered to me at the time, and they were hurtful incidents to a small and not very confident child.

However, as well as being disappointing for me, the events of that sports day were the last straw for my mum, who finally decided to take me away from the school. Quite apart from the fact that I often came home from school upset, she had begun to feel that I wasn't getting a very good education: although I was good at reading, I didn't seem to be learning much else. So she put me in a state school in the hope of enabling me to socialise and have a more relaxed childhood in a rather less strict environment.

Katy Hucker had been my only friend at that school, but when I moved to Yattendon, a middle school in nearby Horley, I began to make some more friends. My cousin Jessica, who was still living with us at the time and who had been going to a different primary school, also moved with me to Yattendon. We were both very shy and so we stuck together and provided some support for each other, which enabled me gradually to start coming out of my shell.

However, by this stage I did have one major problem, which proved to be somewhat of a drawback in my desperate attempts to fit in. I hated boys; not in the way that little girls often say they do, but with a revulsion that led me to throw away anything of mine they had touched. For example, if a little boy used my rubber, it went straight in the bin. It was a deeply felt and very bizarre dislike, particularly considering that I had grown up with four brothers, with all of whom I had very good relationships. If I was told to sit next to a boy in class, I'd say, with all seriousness and with a real sense of anxiety and horror, 'I'm sorry, Miss. I can't. I'm allergic to boys.' Then, if my 'allergy' was ignored and I was forced to sit beside a boy, I'd drag my chair into the middle of the floor, putting as much distance between us as I could.

For the same reason, our country-dancing lessons were regularly punctuated by the cry of some small rejected boy as he complained, 'Miss! Racheal won't hold my hand.'

Unsurprisingly, I began to be teased mercilessly and was eventually sent to see the school counsellor, because it was thought that there must be something seriously wrong at home. But there really wasn't. In fact, my brothers were always extremely protective of me, so perhaps I didn't equate them with other, less kind, little boys.

I still don't know where my extreme dislike of boys came from, but, because it seemed to be shared – and encouraged – by a new friend I'd made at school, it didn't seem particularly odd to me at the time. Always rather a tomboy, I had a very strong perception of myself as a 'horsey girl' with no desire to socialise with boys.

Although always quiet, shy and well behaved, I did have some other very powerful dislikes that developed over the next few years. For example, I had a passionate hatred of jeans and make-up – at least outwardly – and I was adamant that I didn't want to be like the 'cool' girls who held hands with boys, a thought that quite disgusted me.

Every so often there'd be a disco at school and if I was ever persuaded to go to one, rather than getting dressed up in 'cool' clothes, wearing lipstick and putting glitter in my hair like all the other girls, I'd dress from head to toe in my horse-riding gear, complete with riding hat. Understandably, people used to say to me, 'Racheal, why are you dressed like that? It's a party,' and my explanation, which seemed simple enough to me, would be, 'Because I'm a horsey girl, and I'm proud of it.' I was determined not to conform and do all the things most girls of my age did. So again, the other kids had good reason to tease me.

I never felt pretty, and I suppose that, by deciding my identity was firmly rooted in my love of horses, I didn't need to be recognised for what I looked like. It was a statement I made everywhere I went. The only time I ever felt at ease was when I was horse riding, and my riding gear became a sort of security blanket, as well as a barrier that hid me from the rest of the world and protected me from having to compete with and be compared to other girls. Of course, I didn't realise all this at the time; all I knew was that they were the only clothes I felt comfortable in, even at the discos.

In fact, looking back on it now, I always had an issue with clothes in one way or another. For example, all the time I was growing up I'd only wear pyjamas that came right up to my neck and covered me from head to toe. My family just thought I was a bit prudish, but I would almost rather have died than take my top off or get changed in front of the other girls at school. I'm still a bit like that now, in that I always go into a corner to get changed privately at pageants and photo shoots. But, although I didn't consciously realise it at the time, it was an extreme phobia even when I was quite young, and one that caused me a huge amount of distress when I was about ten and we went on a school trip to Wales.

We were away for about five days and all the girls were supposed to shower together every night, in one big shower. But I just couldn't do it, even wearing a swimming costume. It was such a big deal to me that I felt physically sick at the thought.

My best friend at this time was a girl called Belinda, who I'd always thought was very much like me. She also refused to shower with all the other girls, and she confirmed my feeling that to do so would be really disgusting. So, because I took what she said very seriously, I was mortified one evening to hear everyone saying, 'Ooh, Belinda's having a shower in her underwear.' It really disturbed me because it felt so wrong – as though she was doing something 'dirty' and had let me down – and I hid under the covers that night and cried myself to sleep. I'd always thought she felt the same way about things as I did, which made me feel I wasn't completely alone, but suddenly I realised she wasn't like me at all and I felt very isolated.

The next day, when we were all going out on a treasure hunt, I woke up feeling really ill and didn't want to go. I wasn't allowed to stay behind but while we were out I ended up being sick, and so was the first person back to the hostel. I went into the silent, empty dormitory, locked the door, put on my full-length nightdress and stood sobbing under a stream of freezing-cold water in the shower, while everyone else went mad, banging on the door and demanding to come in.

When the door was finally opened I was standing there crying in my soaking polka-dot nightie. Everyone obviously thought I was very strange, and it *was* extremely odd behaviour for a girl of ten. Although not wanting to get changed in public and shower with the other girls might be understandable, it was undeniably peculiar to be so conscious of my body that even with the door locked I felt I had to wear my nightdress because I was terrified that someone might get in and see me.

The thought of having to shower with all those girls felt almost like being raped – that's how serious it was in my mind – and I think when Belinda got into the shower in her underwear it felt to me as though she'd exposed herself. So not only was I traumatised that day, but I also suddenly felt completely alone.

I always avoided anything at school that involved having to change my clothes – swimming, gym, anything to do with sport. Although I didn't think it was odd at the time, I hated my legs and always wanted to wear my tights with my gym skirt, although in fact I'd have preferred to wear my jodhpurs. Because of this, I used to forge notes from my mum to get me out of doing games, and I think I went to only one PE lesson during my whole time at school. One day, obviously suspecting that the note was forged, the PE teacher compared it with the other notes in my file, but of course the handwriting matched up because I'd written all of them. I can't imagine how I came up with all those reasons why 'Racheal is unable to do PE today'.

Even before I left primary school, my apparently determined dislike of all things 'girly' masked a guilty secret. Although always vociferous in my condemnation of make-up, I'd stolen a pot of special prescription camouflage make-up called Dermablend from my mum, which she used to use to cover up some scars on her leg. At the age of 11, I didn't have any spots, but I was convinced I did, and I'd use Dermablend to hide them. I also started to carry around a little palette of red paint from a Christmas cracker, and would never be seen without the red paint on my lips and a thick layer of Dermablend covering my face. Of course at that age I didn't have access to any real make-up, and I suppose I told myself I needed the paint and Dermablend to cover my bad skin rather than for vain, cosmetic purposes.

I remember staying at a friend's house one night and, after washing my face in the bathroom, suddenly realising I'd left my paint palette in her bedroom. Like everyone else, she was completely unaware that I had what I later recognised to be 'appearance concerns', I felt real fear as I tried to work out how I was going to get into the bedroom to retrieve my paint palette without her seeing me. So, looking back on it now, perhaps I was more conscious of my looks than I realised, and perhaps my problems were connected to something a bit deeper than I understood. But at the time I just knew I could never be seen without the paint and concealer, and that having to do so would send me into a panic.

I suppose what I'm really trying to explain is that there were a lot of serious issues even then. What happened later brought out the worst of my illness, but it was certainly already there to some extent. There was so much going on in my head that no one knew about – not even me.

3

Bullied

When I was 12 I moved up to Oakwood Secondary School in Horley, which was when I started to become even more aware of my appearance.

Before I went to Oakwood, I realised that people would think I was a bit strange if I continued to refuse to sit next to boys. Although my dislike of boys was a real phobia to me, similar to the phobia some people have for spiders or heights, I knew I had to do something about it. So the day before school started I told myself, 'Right, tomorrow I'm going to sit next to a boy. I'm going to force myself, otherwise people will think there's something wrong with me,' and in assembly the next day I sat down next to a boy called Stuart Berryman. I was desperate not to make a big deal of it, but inevitably everyone was amazed. Word had already got round that I hated boys and there was immediately a buzz of people saying, 'Look! Racheal's sitting next to a boy,' followed by the predictable poking and general teasing. Not the start I had hoped for.

The scariest thing about secondary school for me was that I'd been split up from my two friends, Fay and Belinda, and put into a class of kids I didn't know. Fay was a really lovely girl, another horse lover, and my best friend. Although I'd always been shy at school, and a very self-conscious tomboy, I never felt awkward when I was with her. But being pulled away from her and put into a class where I had no friends at all made me fall silent, and I virtually didn't speak until I saw her each day at lunchtime.

My crippling shyness was still a problem and, if a teacher told me to stand up in class to read something, I'd feel so sick I'd have to ask to go to the medical room. I simply couldn't do it. I'd sit there each day silently praying, 'Don't ask me to read today,' to the point at which I'd skip lessons rather than risk having to be the centre of attention.

Right from the start I was picked on because of my dislike of boys, but within the first week I began to experience more determined bullying, particularly because of my race. I was frequently hailed with shouts of 'Paki' and asked, 'Ooh, have you been on drugs? You look stoned. Why are your eyes like that?' It was because of my underlying feeling that I was a bit different from everyone else that I had previously resorted to making a definite statement and being completely different. But at secondary school I just wanted to be 'normal' and fit in, although it soon became apparent that I wasn't going to be given the chance.

When I was young I was considered by my family to be a 'pretty little thing' and people used to say, 'Oh, Racheal's going to be so beautiful when she grows up.' Before I was born my mum had drawn a picture of how she thought I'd look, and she says my blue eyes and dark hair were exactly as she'd predicted. It's just sad that the 'design' she'd come up with wasn't what I'd have chosen myself. There may be some truth in what people say about your birth having an effect on what sort of person you turn out to be, as mine was a complicated one by all accounts, with the umbilical cord wrapped three times around my neck! But, despite that, Mum tells me I entered the world looking immaculate, as though I'd cleaned myself up and had a wash, and that, according to all the nurses, I was the best-looking baby they'd seen in six months.

My brother Jason loved photography and had his own darkroom in our house. When I was about five he used to wake me up in the morning and get me to dress up in all sorts of hats and different clothes and take my photograph, at one point entering a photograph of me in the Miss Pears competition. So I think I got used to having my picture taken at quite a young age and that's why I'm quite comfortable with a camera now. But what with that and with everyone's expectations of me growing up to be 'beautiful', when I started to become aware of my appearance I felt I must be a great disappointment to them all. So when the bullying began it just confirmed how I felt and drove home the point that I'd let my family down because I hadn't grown up into the lovely girl they thought I'd be.

Within a month of starting at secondary school, as the bullying and taunts about my looks continued, I went to the market and bought loads of cheap make-up in the most lurid and ridiculous colours imaginable – green, blue and purple eye shadow, thick black eyeliner for my eyebrows, bright-red lipstick and a very white foundation to make my skin as white as possible. Of course, I had no idea how to put make-up on, but as soon as I arrived at school I went to the toilets and just pasted it on lavishly. I must have looked a dreadful sight and, judging from the remarks of all the other kids, I bore a close resemblance to a tart.

As soon as I went into my first lesson, the teacher called me up in front of the class to express her disapproval. 'Racheal,' she told me loudly, 'go and take that make-up off immediately or we'll remove it for you with chemicals.' The class erupted into laughter and I stood humiliated and embarrassed as they called me names, unchecked by the teacher.

Several of the girls in the school's 'popular' crowd wore make-up every day and I had just been trying to fit in, although I realise now that my lack of skill had had just the opposite effect. I was mortified, and I find it hard to forgive that teacher for not taking me aside quietly after the lesson and telling me that my make-up was inappropriate for school.

Eventually I ended up going to school with my bag full of make-up and a big mirror the size of one you'd keep on a dressing table, which meant there was no room in it for any school books or stationery. Throughout the day I'd constantly be looking in this mirror and reapplying my make-up, so it was really no wonder the other kids picked on me. While they were enjoying their break time each day, I'd take my school bag and lock myself in the toilets, get out my huge mirror and apply even more make-up. By this time I'd also started to make repeated checks of my appearance in different lights – daylight, classroom light, hallway light and so on – because I was convinced that they all made me look quite different.

But my experience in the classroom that day also had another effect that was to stay with me for many years to come. It was the first time I realised that people weren't actually bullying me for what I looked like but for what I was making myself look like, which in my mind was quite a different thing and something I could deal with. And that's when I first became aware that I saw my make-up as more of a disguise than something to make me look good. If I applied a mask to my face every day, I could let people say what they wanted, because they didn't know – and therefore weren't criticising – what was underneath.

Another bad day that sticks in my mind was when I went into a music lesson, sat down next to a keyboard and was approached by a girl who said, 'Urgh, I'm not sitting next to her,' as if I was really smelly or repulsive in some way. In fact, I was always very clean, but I immediately felt dirty and so embarrassed; not only did it hurt me very deeply but it also made me feel like a freak. Another time, I was standing in the lunch queue when a girl mistook me for a popular girl and came over and said, 'Oh, Hayley…' She realised her mistake when I turned round, at which point Hayley came over and said, 'Oh, God! Insult!', as if I was really hideous.

That sort of thing happened all the time, and each incident chipped away a bit more at my already very low self-esteem and confidence and made me shrink back even further behind my mask.

Then, when people realised I came from quite a wealthy background, I started to get bullied for that too. I could kick myself now for letting it happen, but kids would come up and say, 'Can I have your dinner money?' and I'd just give it to them. I didn't think twice about it; I'd just hand the money over and then wouldn't be able to buy myself any lunch.

But strangely, although it was probably the worst period of school bullying I ever experienced, it wasn't really hurting me very deeply – at least, not that I was aware of – because I knew that in the evenings and at weekends I'd be at home and riding my horse with Fay. And with Fay as my friend I could cope with it all.

I was picked on by the kids at school because I'm half-Sri Lankan and because I was shy and obviously vulnerable, but Fay was never bullied. She was the sort of girl no one hated. Although she was quiet and calm and didn't really socialise with the others, she was always happy and had a very loud and infectious laugh, and everyone liked her. She studied and worked hard in class, and kept herself to herself most of the time, but she wasn't shy like me.

I think the business of giving away my dinner money was partly because I thought it might make people want to be my friends – there were always kids who wanted to know me because my family was well off. But Fay never took anything from me. Her family was quite poor and she worked really hard for everything she had. At 13 she had one job washing up in a pub, another teaching gymnastics to younger children and another delivering newspapers. I think she wanted to earn everything she owned by her own efforts, and it was always obvious she had the ability and the personality to grow up to be successful. Something I'll never forget is that for one of my birthdays she saved up all her dinner money for a month to buy me a present. Wanting to give like that is a rare quality in anyone, but particularly in someone so young.

Fay and I first met at middle school, when we were eight, and we became friends immediately, brought together initially by our shared love of horses. She was a perfect, really pretty little girl, just like a Victorian doll, with porcelain skin, huge blue eyes, big red pouting lips and golden hair, and she was always laughing and giggling. In fact, I sometimes feel very guilty and selfish when I think about her, because, having had everything given to me and wanting for nothing, I've spent so many years being unhappy, whereas Fay, who came from a much poorer background, had to work hard for everything she had but was always so happy.

She kept me sane and calm and stopped me really caring about what other people thought about me. When things got bad at school and the bullying began to wear me down, I just had to remind myself that I had everything I needed in life and people could think what they wanted.

Fay was the rock on which my whole precarious existence among the kids at school was balanced. She was my greatest friend and the only person outside my own family I felt really comfortable and secure with. In fact, I was probably more at ease with her than with anyone else, because she was my own age and so there were no thoughts I couldn't share with her.

My other friend at that time was Belinda, but, although the three of us were friends together, she didn't like me spending time alone with Fay or anyone else. For example, she'd say to me, 'You're always invited to my house, so if someone else invites you round and you choose to go, I don't want to know you any more.' She really had a hold over me and, after putting a huge amount of pressure on me, eventually persuaded me to leave Yattendon and join her at Reigate Priory Junior School, which is where she went for a while.

Although I had Fay with me at Yattendon, I wasn't having the best time there, and Belinda's insistence left me so emotionally drained that I ended up being unable to cope, crying all the time and becoming so distressed that my mum finally gave in and agreed to let me go to Reigate Priory. But, when I started there, Belinda would just leave me standing crying in the corner of the playground while her new friends tormented me. I'll never understand why they did it, but kids can be very cruel sometimes. Eventually, after a couple of months of feeling really low about myself, I went back to Yattendon – and Belinda followed me.

Although the three of us – Fay, Belinda and I – became good friends, there were several other incidents that I now realise didn't do me much good mentally. For example, when I was about 12 I remember asking Belinda if she could see spots on my face, and her reply was, 'Mmm, only about ten.' Thinking back now, and looking at pictures that were taken at that time, I had none; I still had baby skin and wasn't even starting to get spots, although I was convinced I did have them. So, when Belinda said that, it played on the way I felt about myself and made me feel even worse, reducing still further my already low level of self-confidence. But Fay would always stick up for me; she always protected me, and that was one of the reasons we became so close.

Belinda would also always tell me not to bother working, the way kids do at school. She'd often say, 'If you do that, you're not cool,' and, although I wasn't trying to be 'cool', in our little group of three her opinion was important to me. So I let my schoolwork slide, until one day I found a folder of all the work Belinda had been doing. She'd been studying the whole time and had completed all her projects – and I hadn't.

I'm not blaming Belinda; you never know what's going on in kids' lives that makes them want to take advantage of other children's vulnerabilities. I don't think she got much attention at home when she was young and maybe she was jealous of my friendship with Fay and the closeness we began to have with each other. But I do realise now that the way she treated me when I was growing up probably didn't help my illness.

Having said that, she used to sit patiently outside my bedroom when I was very ill and talk to me through the door, which was lovely. But I do wonder now if perhaps in some way it suited her for me to be locked away in my room, depressed and alone and reliant on her. I realise it must have been very frustrating for her when I wouldn't go out when she wanted me to, but I think she also may have liked the control aspects of our relationship, knowing that I was always going to be there.

I do know how difficult it was for other people when I was ill, and I suppose there were bound to be occasions when they felt resentful. But over the years we've done some press interviews together and the quotes from Belinda have always made me sound really horrible. For example, on one occasion she complained that I didn't even buy her a birthday card any more – at a time when I was locking myself away in my room, self-harming and taking overdoses. She's a very intelligent girl and she knew I was too ill to do anything, even for the people I cared about most, so it did seem to show a lack of understanding on her part.

It's difficult to write about things like this, because I really do want to protect the people I care about. But I thought about it long and hard and decided that if I was going to write the book at all, it had to be honest. The reason I think it's important to say these things is because other people might relate to them and be able to see what's going on in their own lives earlier than I did.

But, getting back to my time at school, when I was 13 the bullying had become so bad that Mum took me out of Oakwood and sent me to school at St Wilfrid's in Crawley – and Fay and Belinda came too. My life improved considerably after that, and, with one or two exceptions, most of the kids there were nice to me.

People used to say that Fay, Belinda and I were triplets, but triplets who were complete physical opposites: Fay and Belinda both had curly blonde hair and fair skin, whereas my hair was dark brown and my colouring was darker. We'd go to school wearing exactly the same clothes, which raised some comments, although most of them not unkind.

But there was one girl at that school who did make me cry. I was in the toilets with Fay one day, looking in the mirror as usual, and this girl was sitting on a bench behind me, constantly making comments. What people didn't realise – and what I didn't realise myself at the time – was that my continual touching up of my make-up wasn't due to vanity, but rather to the desperate need to hide my face. Eventually, I suppose because the girl didn't get the response she wanted, she started to push me, and I ran out crying, fled to the medical room and phoned my brother James and told him what had happened.

James had always been very protective of me and, predictably, he went mad. When we came out of school that day, he was waiting at the gates and walked over to this girl and said, 'What have you been saying to my sister?'

James is very good-looking and it was obvious the girl fancied him. 'Oh, no,' she said sweetly, 'I didn't mean to be nasty to Racheal. She's lovely, a really great girl.' And the problem ended there and then.

Sometimes kids at school are egged on by peer pressure and the desire to follow the gang, and the real instigators of bullying behaviour often keep a low profile and encourage other people to be their mouthpieces. But bullying in any form is never harmless. It can make the kids at the receiving end completely miserable, and can also do serious lasting damage that can affect the rest of their lives. It's something I feel very strongly about because it made me desperately unhappy for a long time, and I never really understood the reasons for it.

4

Bereft

Fay was ambitious, intelligent, hard-working and always cheerful. She had a determination to pay her own way and never to take advantage of other people's generosity that was unusual in someone of her age. She often stayed at my house and I regarded her as my sister, but whenever she came she would save up her dinner money and buy a bag of groceries to give to my mum.

We shared a passion for horses, and the happiest days of my life were spent riding with Fay in the fields around my house. Before I had my horse Freckles, I wasn't allowed to go near the gates at the end of our driveway, let alone set foot outside them. But Freckles had to be exercised, so my parents agreed to my taking her out on the bridle path that bordered our property. However, with Fay riding my Shetland pony, Magic, we would venture far further afield and would use the horses like bikes, riding them to visit friends who lived on an estate some distance away and tying them up outside their houses while we chatted. We would also ride to the local shop to buy sweets, which we'd then take to an orchard to have a picnic. They were wonderful days, full of laughing and joking, and a much-needed and appreciated respite from the trials and tribulations of being bullied at school. But, inevitably, one day we were spotted far from home by one of my mum's friends, and our reckless, but hugely enjoyable, wanderings had to come to an end.

Then, on 13 April 1995, Fay died, and my life changed for ever.

It was a lovely sunny Thursday and we'd been staying with Belinda, messing around at the stables and having a great time, as we always did. We were going to the cinema later that afternoon, and at around 2pm Fay's mother came to pick us up and take us back to my house, where we'd normally have washed and changed together. But when we arrived Fay decided to go home to have a bath, and, although I tried to get her to change her mind, she was insistent. So I let it drop, thinking that, characteristically, she didn't want to take liberties and abuse my family's hospitality. We agreed to meet up again at my house at 4.30, and Belinda and I went upstairs to my bedroom.

When Mum called up to us a little later to say, 'Fay's here,' I went downstairs and glanced at the screen of the security camera before going to meet her at the gate. I was surprised to see that she was climbing back into her mother's Bedford minibus, which drove away again, but I just assumed that she'd forgotten something and was going home to collect it. So I went back upstairs and continued to get ready for the evening.

Suddenly, I felt the most excruciating pain in the pit of my stomach, and a few minutes later heard the loud, eerie wailing of an ambulance siren, which filled me with an inexplicable sense of dread and terrible loss that seemed to press down on my chest and make it difficult to catch my breath. Almost immediately, the phone rang and I could hear Mum's voice as she obviously tried to calm someone down. I felt an overwhelming sense of foreboding but it wasn't until later that I discovered the caller was Fay's mother, screaming hysterically.

I will never forget the moment when my father sat me down and said, 'Racheal, I am so sorry, but Fay has gone.' The pain was indescribable and I felt my world crashing down around me.

I've never understood exactly what happened, but it seems that, when they arrived at my house, Fay and her mother had been arguing, and Fay either jumped or fell out of the minibus, landing on her head and breaking her neck. The accident was reported in the local newspaper, although the details weren't very clear, and perhaps my family kept the full details from me, or perhaps no one ever really knew them. But, although part of me doesn't want to know how Fay died, not knowing has probably made it more difficult to come to terms with her death. I can't bear to think of what her poor mother must have gone through.

It was the most dreadful day of my life, and I still miss Fay so much it hurts. I think of her every day, and remember with pleasure the wonderful times we shared. But it's a pleasure that will always be mixed with a deep and heartbreaking sorrow at the loss of such a unique and special friend.

When someone dies at a young age, people say they were too good for this world, and in the case of Fay Greene I believe that to be true. When Fay was around, it felt as though the sun was shining. She was an angel who was taken away from the world because she was too perfect to remain here.

The day of Fay's funeral was a terribly sad day and I cried uncontrollably until my face was red and burning. She'd always been a practical joker, doing things like falling off her horse and walking on her hands, and up until that day I was convinced – and really believed – that she'd jump out of the coffin laughing. So, when they brought the coffin into the church and she didn't jump out, I was totally crushed. My whole world finally fell apart and it hit me for the first time that she really wasn't coming back.

Later, when they lowered Fay's coffin into the grave, I sat with my legs dangling over the edge of the hole, being close to her for the last time. Even then, I clung to the thought that she was going to jump out, and I desperately didn't want them to fill her grave with earth. I had been absolutely convinced she would be coming home, and it was just so hard to comprehend that she was dead and was never going to wake up.

There were people from school at her funeral, but I almost felt as though I didn't want anyone else there and was selfishly thinking, 'Why are they crying? They haven't lost her. She wasn't their friend like she was mine. They only knew her.'

Although I know Fay's mum was completely distraught, she didn't cry at the funeral at all, and said to me, 'The reason I'm not crying is that I always imagine Fay's with you.' That was the only way she could cope, by telling herself that Fay was staying at my house, as she had so often done.

A couple of days before Fay died, we were sitting on the swing in my garden and she told me exactly what she would want at her funeral. I don't know why we used to talk so morbidly, but I suppose at that age your own death is so remote that discussing it doesn't seem morbid because you don't really think it's ever going to happen. She told me she wanted a horse's head engraved on her gravestone, and talked about a poem and a song by an R&B band called Jodeci that she'd like played during her funeral service. So, although it was horrible to think that what we'd talked about so cheerfully only a few days previously was suddenly so relevant, I told her mum, 'You have to play this song at Fay's funeral,' and was really frustrated when she said she couldn't. In fact, the lyrics were really rude and explicit, although we didn't realise that at the time because we didn't understand them. But she did everything else Fay had wanted.

Some insurance money was paid out as a result of Fay's death, and her mum gave some of it to me, saying that Fay would have wanted me to have it. I used it to buy things to put on the grave, including a lovely plaque of an engraved horse's head, which is still there today, although it's rotting and tucked behind the gravestone now.

I visit Fay's grave every year on her birthday, and know that, wherever she is, she will be remembering me too. When she was taken from me, I felt as though I'd been cut adrift. Her death was a terrible milestone that triggered a downward spiral into emotional despair and psychological and physical illness that ruined my life for several years. But losing her after having had the precious gift of her friendship ultimately taught me that life must never be taken for granted and that you must always make sure you tell the people close to you how much they mean to you.

5

Things That Go Bump in the Night

I sometimes wonder if the house we lived in throughout my childhood may have played at least a small part in the nervousness of my nature because on top of everything else, I had several ghostly experiences there. It was a very large and old manor house in the countryside at Burstow, built in the early 1700s, and it really was quite a spooky place to live.

One of my most frightening experiences occurred after Fay died. I was about to go up the stairs one day when I was suddenly overwhelmed by an icy coldness and saw Fay standing in front of me, dressed in her jeans and zip-up jacket. The last time I'd seen her had been on the security camera as she got out of her mother's minibus at our gates on the day she died, when she'd been wearing a short skirt. And it wasn't until after my experience in the house that I found out that she'd subsequently changed into jeans and a zip-up jacket in the van before she got out of it for the last time and was killed.

But even before Fay died I had some very bizarre and disturbing experiences in the house. For example, one day everyone else was out, my dad was working in the garage and I was doing my homework in my bedroom, when I heard Dad's familiar clomping step coming up the stairs. I called his name but there was no answer, and the footsteps continued across the landing. Then, as I looked towards my bedroom door, I saw a black figure pass by on the other side of its glass panels. Although I knew immediately it wasn't my dad, I shouted his name again and then fled sobbing into the bathroom and locked the door. Terrified and shaking uncontrollably, I crouched there for two hours until Dad eventually found me and confirmed that he had not entered the house at all during the previous few hours.

Those sorts of experiences would have been extremely unnerving for an adult, but, for a little girl who was already anxious anywhere except at home with her family, they were hugely frightening and unsettling.

Occasionally, however, the 'ghostly presence' in the house seemed to show commendable discernment about whom it chose to 'attack'.

After Fay died, I used to invite anyone to the house who would speak to me, because I was very depressed and desperate to have some form of friendship. One day my friend Hannah, her boyfriend and a friend of his called Neil came round and we were sitting together in the kitchen. In fact, Neil was a nasty piece of work and he was trying to persuade me to give him some money. He kept asking over and over again and I kept saying, 'No. I don't want to give you money.' Then, to my horror and distress, he said he knew about the insurance money I'd been given by Fay's mum, so why didn't I give him some of that? I was completely shocked that he could be so cruel and heartless, and just as I said, 'How the hell can you even ask that?', a large cabinet that was screwed firmly to the wall behind him fell squarely on his head. It was quite extraordinary, as though Fay herself had wrenched it free from its attachments and dropped it on him as a sign to leave me alone.

My brothers had strange experiences in the house too, and several other people also said they'd seen a black shadow similar to the one that crossed in front of my bedroom door and frightened me half to death.

When I look back on it now, I realise I spent a lot of time in that house feeling absolutely petrified. The worst of it was that, as my illness became more severe, I wasn't only frightened of the world, but also of being in my own house. I spent an awful lot of time alone in my bedroom when I was ill, but it wasn't just being on my own that made me scared. I was frightened of the room itself, and had an intercom that connected with my parents' bedroom so that I could buzz them in the night if I heard or saw anything.

In fact, I had one of my worst and most terrifying experiences before Fay died, when I was about ten and still in my original room. I had an alarm clock that hadn't worked for ages because its battery was completely flat, and when I was lying in bed one night it suddenly started ticking. I suppose it might be possible for a dead battery to have a surge of power for a few seconds, but it started getting louder and louder, until I realised it wasn't actually the sound of the clock I could hear, but a child's voice saying, 'Tick-tock, tick-tock.' With my heart thumping, I dragged the bed covers over my head and squeezed my eyes as tightly shut as I could get them, dreading what I might see – or what might be able to see me. Almost rigid with fear, I lay there for a few seconds shaking as the sound grew still louder, and then, when I couldn't bear it any longer, I flew out of my bed, through the door and down the stairs to the kitchen. Although I suppose it might have been my imagination, I'm pretty sure it wasn't.

Before my parents bought our house they'd looked at a derelict one down the road, which was eventually bought by the family of a girl called Michelle. The reason it hadn't appealed to my parents was because it had apparently been occupied at some stage by 'devil worshippers' and had a big black puddle on the floor with pictures of devils painted around it. After Michelle's family bought the house, I was there with her in the kitchen one day when I saw the gently swaying top half of the body of someone with long white hair. In a panic, I grabbed Michelle's arm and said, 'Did you see that? Michelle, did you see that?' but she just said, 'No. See what?'

I have wondered if I was just imagining things, or perhaps I have the type of brain that's prone to hallucinating. I obviously do have the capacity to see things that aren't really there, but some of the apparitions were seen by other people too, so maybe they really were there. I'll never know.

It wasn't only in the house that I saw Fay after she died. She used to tell me that if anything happened to her she'd always be riding my horse, and I came out of the house one day, looked towards the paddock and saw her running through the trees, dressed all in white. It was literally only for a split second – there and then gone – and I couldn't really believe what I was seeing, but I suddenly felt an overwhelming calm, which was almost immediately replaced by fear.

I look back now and wonder if it was just my brain replaying the photographic images I had in my head. It's so difficult to accept that someone you loved so much has gone that perhaps you subconsciously daydream about them and can't sort the images in your mind from reality.

Because I could never really believe what I'd seen, I'd come up with all sorts of theories to explain it. I spoke to Fay all the time – and still do – and would sit in my room and keep repeating, 'Please, Fay, show yourself to me if you're here.' Talking to someone in your head like that is a way of keeping them 'alive', and 'seeing' Fay gave me some comfort and the feeling that she hadn't abandoned me but was still at my side and watching over me. Believing *that* meant I wasn't entirely alone.

Another strange experience associated with the house occurred when I was about five and was woken up at 3am by a very loud banging noise that seemed to be coming from the roof. It wasn't a sound I'd ever heard before, and I jumped out of bed in fright and was running towards my parents' bedroom when I met my mum, who shouted, 'Quick, Racheal, run downstairs. We've got to get out of the house. It's on fire.'

My parents and my brothers had all been woken by the same sound that had woken me, which had been followed very shortly afterwards by our Scottish housekeeper thumping hysterically on my parents' bedroom door and shouting, 'Ooh, Jen, my room's on fire!'

As we all huddled together in the garden, shivering with shock, there was suddenly a tremendous explosion and all the windows of the house blew out, showering us with broken glass and releasing a terrifying ball of flames. Minutes later we could hear the screech of the approaching fire engines, although they were too late to save most of our possessions, which had already been reduced to a twisted and charred mass. We were told later that, if we'd remained in the house for three more minutes, none of us would have survived.

Our housekeeper had a room in a part of the house that used to be the servants' quarters, on the same landing as my brothers' rooms, and it turned out that this was where the fire started. I'd gone upstairs to take her something earlier in the evening and, when she failed to answer my knock, I'd peeped through a crack in the door and could see her lying asleep on her bed. As it turned out, it was a sleep induced by a fairly substantial intake of alcohol, and she'd jammed a chest of drawers up against her door to prevent it being opened. But she'd failed to turn off the iron she'd been using earlier, which at some point had fallen or been knocked over and eventually set fire to the house.

Perhaps the most distressing outcome of that fire for me was the disappearance of my kittens, Tabatha and Milo. As we stood watching helplessly as the house burned, I was sobbing and begging my mum to let me go back inside and try to find them, but of course she wouldn't. She kept assuring me they'd have got out, and, although there was no sign of them several days later, I made myself believe that it was true rather than have to cope with their loss and the dreadful thought that they'd been trapped inside and engulfed in the flames. I'd go round the garden every day, calling their names and desperately wishing they'd come home, which, as the days passed, seemed increasingly unlikely. But then, six months later, I went into the garden one day to find them sitting peacefully on top of the shed.

We never discovered what had caused the banging sound that had woken us all up and given us the few extra minutes we needed to evacuate the house safely. But when we were eventually able to go back into the devastation of our home and sift through the mangled remains of our belongings, we found only one undamaged and intact item amid the burned and blackened debris − a framed photograph of Dad's mum.

So, although many of the unexplained events in that house scared me half to death and increased the nervousness I'd always felt as a child, one of them also saved our lives.

6

Learning the Hard Way

I didn't go out for a long time after Fay died, and because I only went back to school for the odd day – which always turned out badly – my education more or less ended when I was 14. I did try very hard to overcome what I suppose was a sort of agoraphobia, and on rare occasions would venture into town when I needed to buy something. But every time I did, kids would throw things at me and shout things like, 'You're ugly,' which reinforced the negative feelings I already had about myself and made it even more difficult to summon the courage to leave my room.

When I stopped going to school, the Social Services sent someone round, but we had large gates at the end of our garden, which were kept locked, and she couldn't get in. It sounds really bad, but Mum didn't push me to go to school. Fay had died, I'd been back to school a couple of times and some teachers had spoken to me in a really unkind was; and I'd taken an overdose, so I think Mum decided my well-being was a lot more important than my education at that time.

As well as feeling overwhelming anger about Fay's death, I also had terrible guilt. I was sometimes cheeky to my parents and was convinced that this had influenced Fay and led to the fateful argument she had with her mother the day she died. As a result I began to be consumed by the thought that maybe she wouldn't have died if she hadn't met me, and it seemed that all the bullying and nasty remarks people made about me were probably justified, and no more than I deserved.

The first time I tried to go to school again was a couple of weeks after Fay died, and, although it was an extremely difficult step for me to take, I was determined at least to try. The first lesson of the day was maths, and I stood outside the classroom for a few moments, trying to force myself to stay strong, before taking a deep breath and walking through the door to my seat. But the one thing I hadn't counted on was that I'd have a clear view of Fay's empty chair across the room. The sight of it was just too much to bear and I burst into tears. The teacher's response was a rather brutal and unsympathetic, 'You should be over it by now,' and I fled from the school and phoned my mum, sobbing, 'I can't go back there. I just can't go back.' It felt as though my whole world had been torn apart and that everyone else was moving on, leaving me totally alone.

After that, Mum was under a lot of pressure from the school to make me attend, and a few weeks later I did try to go back again. I put on fake eyelashes and a mask of make-up and, coincidentally, was in another maths class when I suddenly felt really uncomfortable and wrapped a scarf around my head. The other kids asked, 'What are you doing, Racheal? Why are you hiding your face?' and I said, 'Because I don't want to be seen,' burst into tears and ran out of the classroom. They weren't being unkind and some of them were really sweet, but I didn't realise my behaviour was strange and I couldn't understand why they were making comments.

I went to the medical room and stayed there for a few hours, but, because I really wanted to try to stay in school, I eventually put all my make-up back on and went into a history class. Everyone was sympathetic and asked if I was OK, which made me even more determined to make the effort to stay. There was a boy in the class who was a bit of a joker; he wasn't nasty in any way, and what happened wasn't his fault, but he said, 'Oh, Racheal! What's wrong with your forehead?'

By that time I always wore a cosmetic clay face mask around the house and would coat my face with foundation, so my skin was very dry, and I used to pick at it all the time and make cuts on my forehead. So any skin problems I did have were really self-inflicted. But that was the worst thing that could have happened. As I sat there, feeling like a freak, it seemed as though the whole world was closing in on me, and I could hear the other children laughing as I got up and fled crying from the classroom. I ran out of the school and phoned Mum in tears again, saying, 'I can't go back, Mum,' and then hid in the telephone box for what seemed like hours until she came to get me.

Although I hadn't really been bullied at that school, when that boy asked me what was wrong with my forehead, I suddenly thought, 'Oh, no! He can see what I'm seeing.' Looking back now, I realise he could probably see the cuts I'd made by picking at my skin with my fingernails. But, when he said that, it was the worst I'd ever felt and it made me panic because it absolutely convinced me that other people could see what I saw when I looked in the mirror.

I did go back to school again later to do my mock GCSE in drama, which was really important to me. I was interested in camouflage and theatre make-up and, although I hadn't done any of the course, my mum used to buy me magazines and I had a huge file of cuttings and did my own kind of studying in my room. I was predicted to do well in the exam, and somehow I managed to get through it, although all I can remember is sitting drawing coffins all over the exam paper. Because I had the highest score, I was asked to do the make-up for the school play. I was really excited about it and practised in my room for hours at a time, because it felt as though I finally had a project and something positive to focus on. I was always fighting my fears and was desperate to do better and sort myself out, and this seemed to be a chance to do something I really wanted to do.

Then, the day before the big day, I decided for some bizarre reason that I wanted to dye my hair black, but when I woke up the next morning I didn't like it. Of course, I should never have done it: when you're as ill as I was, changing yourself is really not a good thing to do. But I think I felt that changing my hair colour might make me feel more confident, although unfortunately it had quite the opposite effect. On top of that, I also had a spot on my forehead, which appeared to me to be the size of a golf ball, and the two things together resulted in my having a really bad anxiety attack.

It was awful because the whole school was relying on me and I just couldn't go in. They had no one else to do the make-up and I let them all down and ruined the production. I really hated myself, because I did like all the people at that school – perhaps not the teachers so much, but the kids.

In fact, I once had a really horrible experience with one of the teachers. Even before Fay died, I had a problem with my image of my legs. In particular, I had a real complex about my thighs and would always tie something round my waist to cover them up. It was a Catholic school and you weren't allowed to look untidy, and one day the PE teacher said to me, 'Get that jumper off from round your waist.' So I'd taken it off and was very nervously walking up the stairs, convinced that people would be laughing at my fat legs, when the other PE teacher said, 'Oh, look at you. You think you're it with those tight jeans up your arse!' It was awful;

I felt so embarrassed I just wanted to curl up in a corner and hide, and, looking back, it was an extraordinary thing for any teacher to say to anyone.

I remember on another occasion, when I was having a panic attack about my skin, I told a teacher that I wasn't feeling well and wanted to go home. But he wouldn't let me, and said something along the lines of, 'Oh, you know you're sexy and good-looking,' which was a bit of a sleazy and inappropriate thing for a 40-year-old male teacher to say to a little girl. But you don't realise these things when you're at school; you don't realise that what a teacher may say to you is bad. You just accept it, although I realise now that he shouldn't have been viewing a child of my age in that way.

So, although I think Fay's death may have been the trigger for my downward spiral into really serious illness, I was obviously ill before she died. I was always looking in my mirror and hiding under my hair and was really conscious of my appearance. However, before Fay died, I certainly wasn't ill to the point where it stopped me going to school. I think a lot of teenagers go through a period of having appearance concerns, so mine may have been relatively 'normal' at that time, although presumably body dysmorphic disorder (BDD) was underlying them. Looking back, I realise that the illness was there for a long time to some degree, but unfortunately, as well as some major events like Fay's death, there were also a lot of minor ones that occurred throughout my childhood and increased my feelings of insecurity.

It was shortly after my first attempt to sit through a maths class that I started performing little rituals such as having to touch everything twice. I'd say to myself, 'If I touch that and don't touch it again, someone's going to die,' and if I tried to avoid doing it I'd feel a strong burning sensation in my hand. It was the same feeling you have as a child when someone tells you not to touch something and it makes you want to do it even more. Also, before I went to bed, I'd splash my face with water

30 times, open and shut the wardrobe eight times and check under my bed three times.

They were rituals reminiscent of obsessive-compulsive disorder, although I didn't realise that until much later. All I knew then was that everything had to be a certain way. For example, all the things on the table in my room had to be laid out in a particular order and orientation, and I'd become really upset if anything was moved. I suppose it was because I couldn't control the fact that Fay was gone, but I could control all these other things, and I wonder now if those obsessions became obsessions about my face, which was also something I couldn't control. I think I felt completely powerless with regard to so many things that, as long as I stayed locked away in my room, I could hide from the rest of the world and feel I had control over my life.

7

Solitary Confinement

It was a couple of months after Fay's death when I made my first suicide attempt. I went downstairs when everyone was out and took all the paracetamol I could lay my hands on – I must have taken about 20 tablets. It wasn't a cry for help; I really wanted to die. I began to feel very woozy and sick, and went back to my room and fell asleep. When I woke up the next day I was violently ill and felt an enormous anger because I hadn't died, which only reinforced my feeling that I was useless – I couldn't even get that right.

By this time I'd already started to inhale aerosols, which I was doing fairly regularly and which I'd been introduced to by a friend of mine who told me it would make me drift off into another world. I took great care to hide what I was doing from my family, although they know about it now, and I've never told anyone else about it before.

I'd shut myself away in my bedroom and do what I called 'buzzing' – putting a towel over my mouth to act as a filter, with the aerosol can underneath it, and inhaling until my whole body went numb and I'd hear a 'buzz buzz' sound. It also made me hallucinate and I'd sometimes see Fay in the room. But one of my most frightening experiences was seeing spikes coming out of the ceiling, which got longer and longer and closer and closer until I blacked out, and didn't come round until hours later. It's shocking to think of it now, and of the damage I was doing to my body, but at the time I had no clue about the dangers.

When Mum eventually discovered what I was doing, she realised there was something seriously wrong, but she didn't know what it was or how to deal with it, so she started trying to educate herself and find out about all the things I was going through.

I was also self-harming, but, as I didn't know I had an illness, I didn't realise that what I was doing was a problem. All I knew was that the physical pain I was inflicting on my body helped release the unbearable pain I felt inside and gave me a break from the despair that was always with me. I learned later that physical pain releases chemicals from the brain called endorphins, which enter the bloodstream and act like painkillers, while also inducing a state of euphoria that reduces stress. But all I was aware of then was that digging scissors into my arm, burning myself or cutting myself with a razor somehow dulled my senses and lessened my otherwise unremitting and exhausting misery and emotional distress.

If I got upset enough, I'd have a fit of crying, and then the only thing that made me feel better was cutting myself, although I wasn't aware I was doing it. Sometimes I'd become so angry and get into such a state of panic that I'd black out, and it was only when I came round that I'd see the blood everywhere and realise what I'd done. Then I'd be really worried that Mum would see the cuts on my arms, and I'd have to cover them with a jumper.

Sometimes I'd cut myself when I was out although, again, I wasn't aware I was doing it. I'd go to nightclubs not because I wanted to be out, but because it was a way of accessing alcohol. I'd stand in a corner in the dark and drink as much as I could get hold of, and end up so drunk that I didn't know what I was doing. On one occasion someone saw me and said to a friend of mine, 'Oh my God! I saw Racheal and her whole arm was dripping with blood. She looked really spaced out. I tried to speak to her, but she didn't respond.'

Even when it was dark in a club, people would pick on me and call me names like 'slag' and 'tart' – presumably because of the amount of make-up I was wearing – and I'd go into the toilet, smash a glass and dig it into my arm. I still try to understand why people treated me like that; whatever I looked like and whatever they thought of me, there's no justification for it.

Since that time I've spoken to other people who self-harm, and their experiences are very similar in that they just black out and don't mean to do it. In fact, I think there are two types of people who self-harm: those who do it as a cry for attention, and those who do it to release their inner pain and don't want anyone to know about it.

For me, self-harming was a vicious circle; it made me feel better, but the relief was relatively short-lived and I'd be left feeling completely drained. I always followed the same pattern: lock the door, light a candle, self-harm and go to sleep. When I woke up from the blackouts I'd write graffiti on my bedroom walls – swear words, pictures of coffins, knives with blood dripping off them, wrists being slit or my arm with a mark indicating where I was going to cut it. I'd also draw images of myself – or of how I perceived myself – sometimes with a knife sticking in me, or I'd cut myself and smear the blood across the wall. It was all just horrible, horrible stuff. My room was huge and all the walls were covered in these really awful images and swear words. It was a continuous process – when I was upset I'd write on the walls – and I just can't imagine what was going through my mind. But I was doing it at the same time as I was inhaling the aerosols, so I probably wasn't really with it.

No one saw the graffiti because I never let anyone in my room, but I know my mum went in there eventually, and no wonder she was so concerned about me, although I had no idea at the time what it must have looked like to someone else. We didn't know anything about my illness then, so she must have wondered what the hell was wrong with me, and she said later that she was really scared for me and afraid I was possessed by the devil or something.

It was at about that time that I decided I didn't want to be seen by anyone any more, and for six months I shut myself away in the dark, closed the thick velvet curtains at the windows and didn't even try to leave my bedroom. Mum would put food outside my door and I'd wait until she called up to let me know she was downstairs again before I took it into my room.

If I did go downstairs with my family, I used to be unable to sit and talk to anyone without a mirror beside me all the time, and I'd pick it up repeatedly to do 'light checks' to see whether it was all right for me to be seen in that particular light. My dad feels good when the sun's shining and loves to see it pouring in through the windows, and he'd sometimes say, 'Oh, it's a lovely day! Let's open up all the curtains,' and I'd feel the panic rising and have to run upstairs to hide.

By this time I'd stopped riding Freckles and my parents were becoming desperate trying to take care of her and not really knowing how to do it. They learned what they could about caring for horses, but Freckles needed to be ridden every day and they just couldn't cope. So they ended up having to sell her, which, looking back on it now, was the best thing they could have done. But at the time it filled me with an enormous rage and I hated them for it, not least because of what Fay had once said about always being there riding my horse if anything happened to her.

I have massive guilt about it to this day. I loved Freckles, but I just couldn't bring myself to go out and look after her. I did try, but it meant having to get past everyone in the house and I didn't want anyone to see me, so I'd sometimes go out late at night, after it was dark. But the main problem was that the horse's yard was next to the graveyard and I could see Fay's grave from the stable. That made it even harder, because the pain was as bad as ever, and each time I saw her gravestone it hit me with renewed force that she was dead and that I was never going to see her again, or go horse riding with her or hear her laugh.

I'd sit for hours on the floor of my bedroom, holding my knees and rocking backwards and forwards, repeating over and over again, 'Bring Fay back and take me instead. Why didn't you take me?' I felt that, because her life had been taken, I had no right to have a life, and I also desperately wanted to be with her, which is why I made that first attempt to kill myself.

Already convinced I was seriously deformed, I then developed bulimia. I'd make myself sick if I ate anything at all, and of course eventually became very thin, weighing only six stone at nearly five feet eight inches tall.

Because I insisted on locking myself away in my room, my parents didn't really know what was going on and didn't have any opportunity to check up on me. Dad would sometimes get really frustrated and kick the lock off my bedroom door, but it only resulted in my having a huge panic attack, hurling things around the room and smashing the mirror and everything else in sight. So, because he was afraid of what I might do to myself, he'd be forced to back off. It was really difficult for my parents, because they simply didn't know what to do. They were caught in a trap – if they pushed me into doing things I didn't want to do, they had no idea what I might do next.

I remember asking Dad, in all seriousness, if he'd make a tunnel from my bedroom to the bathroom so I didn't have to come out of the door. In fact, Mum was so confused and worried about what was going on that she eventually agreed to my taking over my parents' bedroom, which had an en-suite bathroom.

Poor Mum knew I was missing Fay and she tried so hard to be understanding and patient, but I took my misery out on the people I loved and could be really horrible. I'd shout at my parents, then go back into my room and cut myself because I felt so bad. It was almost as though I couldn't apologise.

On the bad days, when I couldn't go out – which was most days by this time – I couldn't bear my family to see me either. My parents used to say, 'Look, you're our daughter. We love you no matter what.' But I'd shout at them, 'No, you can't see me. I'm not coming out. Just leave me alone.' Again, if they pushed it too far, I'd fly into a panic and smash things. I hate to say that now, because it makes me sound like such a nasty person, and I did always feel really guilty about being so horrible to them, but, looking back, I realise I couldn't help myself. At the time it just made me feel even worse about myself and increased my self-hatred, and usually resulted in my self-harming.

On one occasion my parents made me leave my room because they wanted me to go to a birthday dinner with them. They were absolutely determined, and Dad forced me to go downstairs. I was in a terrible panic, kicking and punching, and I punched an old glass cabinet and cut my hand really badly. I think it was at that point they realised just how serious things had become. Although Mum knew I was grieving over Fay's death and tried really hard to support me while I came to terms with it, after that incident she took me to see the doctor and I was referred for an appointment with a psychologist. But the appointment was taking so long to come through that she eventually rang the mental health centre and begged them to see me, and I was given an appointment with a counsellor.

Mum didn't know what was wrong with me, but she never

wanted me to take anti-depressants because she didn't want me to go down the same road she'd gone down when she became addicted to them when I was younger. She was sure that what I needed was to find the right counsellor – but it was finding the right one that was going to be the problem.

Of course, to be able to see a counsellor I had to leave my room, which Mum only managed to persuade me to do a couple of times, particularly because when I went for the first session I didn't like the way the counsellor tried to relate my problems to something in my childhood. It wasn't her fault; she didn't have any more idea about BDD than we did – very few people did at that time – but I became very angry. She asked me about my life at home and about my relationships with my brothers, and I thought, 'No. You've got it all completely wrong.' I knew what she was implying, but I was really close to my brothers and really upset by the suggestion. So after a couple of times I refused to go again.

It was also hard because I'd be up and down: there'd be a day when I'd try to face the world for something like that, and then days when nothing would get me out of my room and, if I couldn't leave my room, I couldn't keep an appointment with a counsellor. It might have worked if it had been possible for her to come and see me, although she'd have had to be prepared to talk to me through the closed bedroom door. In fact, I think there are options like that today, but they weren't available at that time; I either had to go to her place, or not at all.

Mum must have been distraught by this point. I think she'd pinned all her hopes on the idea that counselling would help me, so when that failed she decided to enrol in a counselling course herself. She was desperate to find out anything she could about my problems, and I suppose she thought, 'Well, if Racheal won't go to a counsellor, the counsellor [Mum] will have to go to her.' It was after Mum did that counselling course that she decided the only option left was to throw me in at the deep end.

As I say, I had good days and bad days; the bad days were the days on which I wouldn't leave my room at all, and even the good days weren't what most people would call 'good'. Normally I'd give Mum a list of anything I wanted and she'd go out and buy it for me. But after the counselling sessions I did start trying to venture out again, although only for really important things.

I'd begun to wear a cosmetic clay face mask all the time, because it meant I didn't have to put on all the make-up and fake eyelashes. I was convinced I had really bad acne, although in fact the face mask probably *caused* skin problems in the end, but it did enable me to go downstairs for dinner. After a while the mask became too much, and I made myself a Muslim-type veil out of an old tea cosy and a piece of material, which was much better because it allowed my skin to breathe more easily.

Eventually I advanced from wearing the full face mask or veil when I was around my family and the people I loved to sometimes putting big white blobs of face mask or talcum powder all over my face to cover what I imagined were my terrible spots. The blobs allowed me to breathe better than I could when my whole face was covered, and I thought that, if people were looking at them, they wouldn't be looking at me. We had lodgers at that time, and they must have thought, 'What on earth is wrong with this girl?' But no one ever said anything. No one really knew I was suffering from an illness; they simply thought, 'Oh, that's just Racheal being Racheal.'

I kept begging Mum to take me to the doctor to get something for my acne, and when she eventually did, the doctor said, 'Racheal, you don't need anything. We can't prescribe anything for you,' and on another occasion a doctor asked me, 'Have you tried using Dove soap?'

I was really angry at their refusal to give me anything for what I saw as a really disfiguring problem, and I'd think miserably, 'Why is everyone against me? Why can't they see?' It's like seeing a massive boil in the middle of your forehead and everyone telling you it isn't there. When I looked in the mirror, I was covered in acne, and not just a few spots – my face was completely disfigured. Of course, the fact of the matter is that people who do have bad acne manage to carry on normal lives, but to me it was an insurmountable (although imagined) problem.

I really did try very hard to go out and it was always extremely disappointing and frustrating when I didn't manage it. I'd say to friends, 'Look, come round and I'll definitely come out,' but they'd end up sitting outside my bedroom door while I stayed in my room sobbing and having a panic attack. Needless to say, it was impossible to maintain friendships when I couldn't see anyone, and I eventually lost almost all my friends.

I became completely self-obsessed – not the kind of person anyone would want to be friends with, because all I talked about was myself. Anyone who had any kind of relationship with me had to live their whole life around me and how I was feeling. I used to feel so angry, not only because I hated what I looked like, but also because I hated who I'd become: I was furious with myself for being so concerned about my appearance and caring so much what people thought about me. To this day I don't know why I felt like that, but it was completely out of my control, and very painful and miserable to have to try to come to terms with it.

The only time I felt relatively content was when I was sitting in my room in the dark, very often with candles burning and listening to music. When we were younger, Fay and I made a tape of ourselves pretending to run a radio station, and it included Fay singing 'Frere Jacques', which I listened to over and over again. It was only when I was alone in my room that I could cope with the way I looked. The panic attacks would start if I had to get ready for something. If someone said, 'Racheal, you have to go here,' or 'You have to come out of your room,' I'd think, 'OK, I'll try,' because I really wanted to go out. But then I'd feel even worse because I just couldn't do it. Of course, I'd never heard of BDD at the time, and had no idea that was what I was suffering from, or, indeed, that I had any type of illness.

One of the worst days during that time occurred when my brothers sneaked into my room and took away all my make-up and my hair diffuser. They were obviously very concerned about their little sister using so much make-up at such a young age, and about the fact that I was hiding myself away all the time, and they thought that removing my make-up would stop me wearing it. When I discovered it was missing, I was completely overwhelmed by panic. My brothers kept saying, 'No, we haven't taken it,' and I just couldn't cope. I went absolutely ballistic and smashed everything up, and I think that's when they first realised I wasn't simply being overindulged by my parents; I was really ill.

A BDD attack is really a panic attack. I'd get really anxious and feel as though I couldn't breathe, and then everything around me would begin to spin and go black, and I'd start pulling at my hair, completely lose control and become really angry. I'd often end up beating myself up or smashing things in my room, and when I eventually came out of those episodes, I'd find I'd cut myself. I don't really remember the rages; I just remember the mess afterwards. Something in my brain would switch off and I'd completely lose it, and then it was like waking up from some sort of blackout.

One of the triggers of the attacks was trying to put make-up on to go somewhere and not being able to make it perfect, the way I wanted it; the frustration would be just too much to bear. It was such a massive, time-consuming and exhausting ritual that I was devastated if at the end of all that it went wrong. It was really disappointing as well, because if a friend wanted me to go to the cinema, I'd be excitedly looking forward to going out and then, after spending many hours getting ready, it would all go wrong and I wouldn't be able to leave my room. I'd feel that my face was stopping me doing what I wanted to do, so I'd take out my frustration on my face, and on myself.

I hated doing all that preparation, but there was no alternative; I *had* to do it. What I hated most about it was that I was so concerned with it. Why did I care so much? What did it matter what people thought? But I just couldn't help being concerned about what people thought of me.

It seems very strange now, looking back on it, because I can't really believe I was ever like that. It's almost as though I'm talking about someone else, some poor girl I can't help feeling sorry for.

Having originally gone out in my disguise and been able to cope with the mickey-taking because I felt it was directed at my carefully contrived outward appearance, I eventually started to feel that my disguise *was* me. So I'd take people's comments a lot more personally, which made it even more difficult for me to leave the house – or even my bedroom – and for a long time I very rarely went anywhere at all.

I suppose wanting to look peculiar started at a young age, when I used to wear my horse-riding gear all the time, but it gradually developed into something far deeper and more debilitating. There's a huge difference between being concerned about what you look like and allowing those concerns to disable and control your life, which is the point I'd reached by this time.

I went through so many phases. As well as the 'horsey girl' disguise, there was another stage when I dressed like Dracula and another when I looked like a drag queen – completely over-the-top, ridiculous make-up with bright-red lipstick. It wasn't make-up like most people wear; it was thick layers of concealer, foundation, powder, concealer, foundation, powder. I used to put on anything I could lay my hands on, and as much of it as possible, and I wanted any product that was available to add to my disguise.

I look back now and think, 'Why was I doing that?' I suppose it was another way of trying to divert attention away from the real me. If I'd gone out without any make-up on and someone had said, 'Look at you. You look disgusting,' I'd have known they were criticising *me*. But if I went out dressed as a complete freak, I could think, 'Well, it's only my disguise they're saying that about. I can live with that.' Criticism and cruel comments were much harder to take if they were directed at what I actually looked like rather than at what I made myself look like. So I think that's probably why I went through all those different stages. I sometimes wonder if the Goths of today are doing a similar thing – compensating for feeling insecure by wearing clothes and make-up as a mask so that people focus on those rather than on the person underneath.

But underlying it all was the fact that I hated myself. I hated my appearance and I hated *who* I was, because I couldn't control it. Because of my overwhelming feelings of self-loathing, I would sometimes look in the mirror and punch myself in the face, taking out on myself my rage at being trapped in my body, and it became a vicious circle from which I couldn't break free. I didn't have Fay any more, and so I felt there was no one who could take the pain away. There was no one who could help me, and no one knew what was wrong with me. Everything was spiralling out of control and yet I didn't have any idea that I was actually ill.

No one knew about the self-inflicted bruises on my face, because they never saw me without make-up, the face mask or the veil, but one day Mum bought me a punch bag so that I could take out my aggression and anger on that. It was a good idea, but it used to swing back and hit me, and probably hurt *me* more than I hurt it.

Mum didn't know I was cutting myself either, until the sleeves of my jumper fell back one day and she saw the marks on my arms. I can remember the look of absolute shock and disbelief on her face and the distress in her voice when she said, 'Oh my God! What is that?' She was really upset and obviously very frightened when she realised how serious things were.

8

Living With Fear

Even when I really wanted to go out, I usually just couldn't
do it. My friend Belinda would come round and sit outside
my bedroom, patiently talking to me through the door, and one
day she eventually managed to persuade me to go with her to an
under-18s disco. It was somewhere my parents would never
normally have let me go, but, as I'd hardly been out of my
bedroom in the six months since Fay's death, they were so anxious
for me to go *somewhere* that they were prepared to agree to it.
Although at this stage I wasn't as ill as I became later, I would only
go to dark places, which is why the disco was a possibility.

Walking into the club, I felt as though everyone was staring at
me and whispering behind my back. I'd covered my face with the
thick layers of make-up I always wore, which had become the
mask I showed to the rest of the world, and as soon as we arrived
I started looking in the mirror. It wasn't long before a girl said to
me, 'Oh, look at you. You love yourself.' I can see now why people
must have thought that, but the reality was completely the
opposite. Then suddenly this girl grabbed hold of me and smashed

a glass into my face, gouging a deep cut across my eyebrow and spattering blood everywhere. Fortunately, my friends jumped on her and pulled her off me before she could cut any deeper, because I didn't put up any sort of a fight, but just lay there on the floor feeling empty and detached. What did it matter if she beat me to death? I wanted to die anyway. But then I caught a glimpse of my blood-covered face in the mirror and was suddenly terrified.

The bouncers took me outside and called my mum, and everyone was panicking because there was so much blood on my face they couldn't tell how badly I was hurt. Mum took me to hospital, where they cleaned me up and put several stitches in the cut – and that was the end of my going out at night, because the terrible fear I already had was now compounded by the new fear of being physically attacked.

Some of the girls involved in that attack did apologise to me later. Maybe their dislike of me was fuelled by their perception that I was a stuck-up little rich girl, although I wasn't like that in reality. I did try to make friends, but people just wouldn't accept me the way I was, so that was that.

Shortly after that incident, Mum went out with a friend of mine to see if she could identify the people who'd attacked me. Eventually, she found them outside the shopping mall in town – at which point my friend made a hasty exit and phoned me in a state of panic to tell me what Mum was doing.

Small as she is, it takes quite a lot to daunt my mum, and apparently she went right up to this group and asked, 'Do you know somebody called Racheal Baughan?'

One of them said, 'Yeah, that stupid slag. She thinks she's it.'

Mum was furious. 'Well, I'm her mum,' she said, 'and I'd like to ask you something. How did you feel after you'd done that to her?'

A boy answered, 'Huh, she deserved it. Anyway, she's a weirdo. She didn't even defend herself.'

Resisting the urge to send him flying through an adjacent plate-glass window, Mum gave them all a piece of her mind and told them I was ill and very unhappy.

One of the girls in that gang was a pretty, half-Italian girl who'd always taken any opportunity to bully me whenever she saw me. But not long after Mum had confronted them, I went out one day and, as usual, people were jeering at me and shouting abuse, and this girl came over and had a go at them, telling them to leave me alone. Then she turned to me and said, 'Just go, Racheal.' She nearly got into a fight trying to protect me, and after that she stopped hanging round with them. You have to be impressed by someone who can change her attitude like that, particularly because it takes a lot more courage to stand up for yourself rather than just follow the crowd.

My fear of going out was reinforced still further by another disturbing experience I had when I was about 14. It occurred on one of the rare occasions when I'd managed to pluck up the courage to venture out to a friend's house one evening to watch a video. She didn't have much food in the house and, as I was starving, I decided I'd go to the nearby shop and buy us some sweets and crisps.

Although I was very nervous as I walked the short distance to the shop, it was dark and quiet and I was sure I could get there and back without being seen. However, as I approached the shop I saw a gang of around 30 kids hanging around outside it, some of whom I recognised as kids who made a habit of taunting me. But, feeling the panic rising inside me, I forced myself not to turn and run, and continued to walk slowly towards the relative safety of the shop, with my hair over my face in the hope that no one would recognise me.

Suddenly one of them turned round and saw me and shouted, 'Oi, Paki,' and then the whole group joined in with cries of 'Go away, freak.' I froze in my tracks; although I desperately wanted to run, I simply couldn't make my feet move. Rooted to the spot and with my heart pounding, I then noticed in horror that one of the gang was holding a baseball bat, and it was at that point I heard someone shout, 'Your mum's a fucking Paki. Get out of here. You're rough.' The cry of 'Your mum's a Paki' was then taken up and chanted by the rest of the gang.

As much as it hurt when people said awful things about me, a part of me felt I deserved them. After all, I did look like a freak and they were just confirming everything I already felt about myself. But saying things about my mum was a different story. She didn't deserve their disrespect and dislike. What had she done wrong? They'd gone too far, and for the first time in my life I was ready to stand up to them. Furious, I started to walk towards them. I had no idea what I was going to do, but as I drew nearer I shouted, 'Don't you ever say things like that about my mother. Take it back.'

Inevitably they just laughed, and the taunts continued as they moved en masse towards me, the boy with the baseball bat wielding it with the obvious intention of attacking me.

Then suddenly, out of the blue, a woman came down the road and stood firmly in front of me, facing my would-be attackers. 'Keep away from her,' she told them angrily, 'or I'm calling the police.'

After standing around for a few seconds, they obviously realised it was best to take her threat seriously and they all ran off, jeering and calling over their shoulders, 'We'll get you next time, Paki.'

With the anger drained out of me, I was left crying and shaking as my rescuer held me in her arms. She told me that when she saw me standing there it reminded her of her little girl, who is half-Asian, and she wasn't going to stand by and watch what happened. Then she walked me back to my friend's house to make sure I got there safely, and my mum came immediately to pick me up and take me home.

It was an experience that left me deeply disturbed and upset, and if it hadn't been for that woman I dread to think what would have happened. But in one way I didn't care; what would it have mattered if they'd killed me? All I knew was that no one could speak about my mum that way and, although terrified, I'd protect her with my life.

Looking back, I can see why it was so difficult for me to try to make myself face the world. It was a Catch-22 situation, as not only was I mentally ill with BDD, but also every time I did try to take a step forward and force myself to leave the house, something dreadful would happen to knock me back again.

Although I was still grieving after Fay's death, I gradually began to want to have a life again. But by that time I felt as though my body was a prison in which I was trapped; it was holding me back from being able to do the things I wanted to do and to be the person I wanted to be. I dyed my hair very black and a hairdresser came round to the house to give me a perm, and when I really wanted to go out I'd have a bath, put masses of make-up on and do everything I could think of to disguise my looks. I had a whole ritual of getting ready, which took about five hours. But, having done all that, if I still didn't like what I saw in the mirror, I'd think, 'No, I can't. I can't go out,' and the whole five hours would be wasted and I'd feel even more depressed than before.

Part of my ritual was doing my make-up, which all had to be done a certain way. I'd put big ticks of eyeliner going up from the corner of each eye, and, if one tick didn't turn out right, I couldn't go out. If my eyes watered and the make-up wouldn't stay in place, I couldn't go out. If I thought I had a big spot, I couldn't go out. Only on the days when I thought I'd covered my spots and my eye make-up was just right could I at least try to face the world.

Applying my make-up was a lengthy and exhausting process – both physically and mentally – that took me at least an hour and a half. It was rather like painting a canvas: if the paint didn't go on to the canvas properly, I couldn't be seen; but, if the paint was right, I could try to leave my room. It wasn't about trying to look glamorous; my make-up was an essential mask that had to be applied correctly before I could even think about leaving my bedroom.

When things didn't go right, it would trigger an anxiety attack which would often end up with me self-harming, or worse. Perhaps the best way to try to explain what it was like is to describe one particular day.

I woke up one morning feeling pretty good and opened the thick, dark curtains that completely covered my huge bedroom window. That in itself was a rare thing for me to do, as I normally kept the curtains tightly closed so that my room was permanently pitch black. But on this particular day I'd woken up feeling I really wanted to try to venture out to the shops, and as the sun came flooding in through the window I felt a surge of optimism that I'd be able to face the day.

I began my usual ritual by delving into my large make-up bag and removing and carefully polishing each item of make-up before displaying it in strict order on the dressing table – eyes, lips, face, concealer, blusher, fake nails, fake eyelashes and so on. Next I gathered together all the things I needed for a bath: Aquis Cream to wash my sensitive skin; a new clean razor; clay face mask; exfoliator; Aussie Shampoo and 3 Minute Miracle conditioner; bath salts; and the small mirror I kept face down beside the bath so that I could constantly check the progress of my skin throughout my bath sessions.

After having spent an hour and a half cleaning myself, shaving my legs, putting on the face mask, exfoliating and doing all the other things that were part of my ritual, my skin had begun to flare up and I returned to my bedroom feeling the first stirrings of anxiety. Looking back on it now, it was hardly surprising that my skin became red and blotchy after I'd spent more than an hour in a hot steaming bath performing my obsessive ritual of putting on a face mask, washing my face 30 times and then exfoliating. But, trying to ignore my feeling of unease, I continued to get ready.

First I covered my body in cocoa butter before starting to examine my 'fat legs' and visualise cutting away my thighs. I extended one leg and shook it, fighting the feeling of nausea as I watched the flab move back and forth, and then continued to study both legs in minute detail. Disgusted by the sight of all the ugly blue veins that showed through their paper-thin covering of translucent skin, I felt my heart sink as I realised just how abnormal my legs were. Forcing myself to continue, I began to rub cocoa butter over my stomach and had to fight the revulsion I felt as I imagined the fat moving around beneath my hand.

Two hours into my ritual and determined to persevere, I put my pyjamas back on, tightened the towel around my hair and turned to face the mirror. As usual, the mirror was placed directly in front of daylight so that I could ensure my disguise was adequate in the most unforgiving and revealing light of all, which was the one I was most fearful of. Although I loved the sunshine when I was younger, getting my disguise to go right was even more difficult in hot weather, as I had a terror of it melting and deteriorating much more quickly than normal.

I started by covering my face with tinted moisturiser and, once that had soaked in, picked up my Boots Number 7 cream concealer and pasted it liberally all over my face and neck. When that had dried to a powdery consistency, I applied Cover Girl liquid foundation before touching up my spots again with an anti-bacterial cover-up stick. The final step to complete the base was to dust my face with very white powder and then go over it again, dabbing it with talcum powder on a make-up sponge to make sure it was white enough. I'd read somewhere that you can make your nose appear smaller by using a brown pencil to draw on it the nose you want and then blending it down the sides before filling in the middle with a light concealer. So I completed this technique next, in the hope of camouflaging and concealing my dreadful nose.

However, on this particular day my disguise just wasn't working and I could feel myself getting hotter and hotter and could still clearly see my red, spotty skin showing through. But despite the heavy feeling of sickness that had settled in my stomach, I was determined to continue in the hope that things would improve by the time I'd completed all my preparations. So, picking up my black eyeliner, I drew thick, dark lines over my eyebrows until they were just a little less than an inch wide, concealing the scar on my right eyebrow that I'd been left with after having a glass broken in my face.

Next I turned my attention to reshaping my horrible big round eyes. I began by applying an eyelid base with a creamy powder consistency. Then, once that had dried, I added liquid black eyeliner, starting from the inner corner of my eye and taking it out to the far side, just below the end of my eyebrow, in a sort of Egyptian style. I ran the line all the way along underneath my eye before going over the imperfect bits with a damp cotton-wool bud. Then I applied thick, black eye shadow to each eyelid, blending it in stages with lighter shades of brown up to the eyebrow, and added highlighter just below the brow line. Once all the shading was in place, I put on long, thick, black fake eyelashes. The glue was getting everywhere, but I persisted until the eyelashes were in place, although by this time my eyes were watering like crazy and ruining my Egyptian line, and the panic started to set in.

With my anxiety increasing by the second, I sucked in my cheeks and started applying cream blusher in such a way as to give the illusion of high cheekbones, a trick I'd learned from cuttings from the various magazines I'd saved over the years. Then I finished off with a dusting of bright-red powder blush to draw attention away from my round face, and applied highlighter just above the blusher line along my cheeks before starting on my lipstick. Having put on a base coat and concealer to make my lips look fuller, I picked up my dark-plum lip liner and reshaped my horrible thin lips with a thick line to create the illusion of a pout. I then filled in with dark-plum lipstick, blotted with tissue and repeated the whole process seven times before adding thick, dark lip gloss to complete my disguise.

To me this was not merely make-up: it was a canvas that had to be painted perfectly before I could face anyone. As I sat looking in the mirror, a deep sense of disappointment began to creep over me when I realised that the freak was still showing through my disguise. 'Why isn't it working?' I screamed at my reflection, grabbing a pair of scissors and digging them into my arm. Immediately I felt a slight easing of the tightening sensation in the pit of my stomach as the physical pain took over, and, taking a deep breath, I continued with my ritual.

After running a comb through my wet, permed, dyed-black hair, I coated it with three handfuls of mousse and, tipping my head forward, dried it with the diffuser of the hairdryer. Then, as I sprinkled water over the top of my head to style my hair into place, I realised the curls weren't all the same. Everything was starting to go wrong. I'd already spent four hours getting ready and, as it was now around 4pm, it was looking increasingly unlikely that I'd make it to the shops before they closed. But I still refused to give in, and continued with my preparations, clinging desperately to the hope that I could correct all the defects and still manage to face the day.

Shaking with anxiety, I tried to apply glue to my nails, but the fake nails kept flicking off and I ended up with glue all over my hands. I could feel hot tears of frustration and disappointment pricking my eyes. 'Don't cry,' I told myself firmly. 'You'll ruin the make-up.' But I couldn't help it. I felt useless and defeated and the misery started to overwhelm me as I screamed and threw the nails across the room.

Looking in the bathroom mirror, I could see to my horror that I was already deteriorating and that my disguise was melting and revealing my face. I felt trapped and desperate as I reached for a razor and cut into my arms. Although the physical pain did help a bit, the internal pain just wouldn't go away and I started to punch myself violently in the face, screaming, 'Why have I been punished with this face? What did I do that was so bad? If there is a God, please take me. I can't bear it any more. Please take me away and set me free from this body.' As I struggled to breathe, I felt an agonising pain deep in my stomach and everything around me became blurry. My head was spinning as I sank to the floor and sat rocking backwards and forwards, screaming out the same words over and over again.

Not knowing how much time had passed, I eventually stood up, picked up a heavy Christian Dior perfume bottle and hurled it into the mirror again and again until the glass smashed. Then, turning my attention to the perfectly ordered items on the shelves lining my bedroom walls, I knocked them all to the floor with one sweep of my arm. Although dimly aware of the blood dripping from my arm, I couldn't stop myself. The only thought in my head was that I couldn't bear this body and this face any longer and, knowing that I was alone in the house, I sneaked downstairs to look for something to relieve the pain.

By this time my parents had started hiding all the tablets from me, so there were none to be found anywhere. I ran hysterically around the house searching desperately and punching myself all over my body, screaming, 'Please take me away. Please. I can't bear it any longer.' Finally I found some tablets hidden at the back of Mum's underwear drawer and, as the relief flooded over me, I poured them down my throat followed by the water in a glass on Mum's bedside table.

Suddenly calm, I walked back down the stairs, took another look in the mirror and tried one last time to readjust my disguise, but I still couldn't make it work. Nausea and exhaustion washed over me as I flopped on to my bed and tried to comfort myself with the thought that it would soon all be over and I'd be with Fay. I prayed that my body wouldn't follow me into the afterlife and that I'd soon be at peace, and the pain and despair finally began to slip away as I fell into a deep sleep.

It was about 10pm when I woke up and pinched myself in disbelief, unable to understand how I could still be alive. As the reality hit me and I sat up, a sudden wave of nausea had me running to the bathroom. But it was too late, and I was violently sick on the way. Feeling weak and completely defeated by misery, my only thought was that I was so useless I couldn't even manage to kill myself, and, instead of finding the peace I longed for, I knew I'd have to try to face another day.

There were times when I did manage to go out, but I was absolutely petrified and my heart would be pounding and I'd have dreadful stomach cramps. I think now that there were a lot of aspects of agoraphobia – as well as paranoia and obsessive-compulsive disorder – in my illness. I was convinced I could hear people laughing and giggling about me all the time. Whether they were or not, I'll never know, because my overwhelming feelings of shame and self-hatred made me walk with my head down and my hair covering my face, so I couldn't see if people were actually mouthing the words I heard or whether they were in my head. However, I know that at least sometimes I wasn't imagining what people were saying, because the bullying was real enough and in fact one episode was caught on camera when I was taking part in a documentary a few years ago.

Everywhere I went I could hear people shouting, 'Oh, look at that girl. She's so ugly.' I'd hear little kids saying to their mothers, 'Oh, look, Mummy. Look at that girl's nose.' I think most of those voices probably *were* in my head, but I was convinced I could hear them, and the fact that similar things had been said directly to me by other kids at school and by kids in town didn't help me to sort out reality from imagination.

So, on the rare occasions when all the preparations went right and I'd managed to do my make-up exactly as I wanted it and was able to leave my room, I felt that people were laughing at me and saying, 'Oh, look at her! She's a freak!' Some of them probably were, because I'd wear a long black coat, loads of make-up and thick black eyeliner, and, understandably, people started calling me Dracula.

I had lots of those long black coats, because, if there was something I liked, I'd get Mum to buy me several exactly the same. It must have been very hard for Mum, because people would say, 'Oh, she shouldn't feed Racheal's illness,' but what else could she do? She didn't know what was wrong with me and she didn't know how to help me, so all she was really able to do was try to keep me calm by going along with the relatively harmless things I asked her to do.

Eventually, the only place I would ever go was into Crawley with my mum, and one day, when I was about 15, she managed to persuade me to go out with her so that she could buy me some clothes. While we were there, we bumped into my sister-in-law, and, as we were standing talking to her, a young woman passed by pushing a small child in a pushchair. As she drew level, she said something like, 'Ugly bitch,' and I immediately started to shake and cry and begged Mum to take me home. But Mum was absolutely furious. She left me with my sister-in-law and went storming off after this woman; she told her that I was ill and that she should try to imagine someone saying something like that to her own little girl. She really tore a strip off her.

By the time she came back, I was in a real panic and said, 'Oh my God, Mum! Do you know who that was? She's got a reputation as being the toughest girl in Crawley. She's really hard.' Needless to say, we had to go home, and all Mum's careful preparations and persuasion to get me out of the house were wasted.

But it had a very unexpected outcome in one respect. The following day, when Mum went back to the town centre to buy me the things we'd originally gone out to buy, the woman came rushing up to her, flung her arms around her and said, 'I'm so sorry. I thought about what you said yesterday and I know how awful I would feel if that happened to my daughter. Please forgive me.'

I do have respect for someone who can do that, who can realise what they've done and admit it to themselves and apologise. Perhaps sometimes people who are bullying just need educating. Maybe they're afraid to go against the group because they feel people will turn on them instead.

There was the occasional silver lining to the dark clouds we all lived under during those years, the most important of which occurred when I was 15. Very ill and still very much grieving for Fay, I started to have dreams about my brother Andrew. Although I'd continued to miss him over the years, I don't think I'd realised just how much of an effect losing him had had on me. The dream was always the same: I went downstairs to find my family gathered around the dining table having a big roast dinner, and there, sitting among them, was Andrew. I'd run towards him to throw my arms around him, only to realise at the last moment that he was in a cage and I couldn't touch him. The dream recurred for about a month, and when I eventually told my mum about it, she was obviously very concerned.

Then one day, when I was sitting as usual in my darkened bedroom, Mum called me down for dinner. 'I can't come out of my room today,' I told her. 'Can you please leave it outside my door?'

'No, not today,' she said. 'I've got a surprise for you.'

Under normal circumstances, I wouldn't have left my room for a million pounds on a day when I felt bad, but for some reason I had an instinct that the surprise was something important. So I grabbed my bottle of talc, put big white blobs all over my face and made my way nervously down the stairs.

As I entered the kitchen, a tall, handsome man was standing in front of me, looking rather like a taller version of Tom Cruise. It took me a few moments to realise who it was but as recognition began to dawn, he said, 'It's Andrew,' and, with tears pouring down my face, I threw my arms around him. It felt as though a huge empty space in my life had suddenly been filled. (He didn't even mention the blobs on my face; perhaps he didn't really notice them because he was as happy to see me as I was to see him.)

We have a wonderful relationship again now; he's moved into the house next door to my parents and often attends my parties in London. One of my greatest enjoyments in life is having my family around me, and so I'm eternally grateful to have Andrew back. I think the loss of Fay taught us all that life is too short to hold a grudge, and being reminded of that was perhaps what made my parents willing to put the past behind them and make a fresh start with Andrew. Although the gap left in my life by the loss of Fay can never really be filled, having Andrew back went some way towards easing the pain, and it made me realise how important it is to show the people you love what they mean to you and never to take them for granted.

Shortly after we welcomed Andrew back into the family, I started to think a lot about my big sister Jennifer. One day, when I was going through an old photo album, I became mesmerised by all the photos of her and tried to visualise what she'd be like now. When I'd last seen her she'd been tall, about five feet ten, with long blonde hair and beautiful blue eyes – the perfect idol of a big sister.

Suddenly I decided I'd write her a letter. I didn't want to tell my parents about it, as I knew how much heartache their argument had caused, but I just wanted to make sure she was OK. It wasn't until I'd finished writing the letter – which I illustrated with a picture of me as a little girl – that it dawned on me that I didn't know where she lived. Much to my disappointment, all I could do was put the letter away in my drawer in the hope that I'd eventually think of a way to obtain her address. But, after an unsuccessful Internet search and a fruitless call to directory enquiries, I was giving up hope.

However, unknown to me, my mum had already come across the letter in my drawer and shown it to Dad. Apparently, they were both deeply touched by what I'd written, and Dad decided enough was enough and it was time to pull the family back together. Dad doesn't know much about computers, so Mum helped him to track Jennifer down on Friends Reunited, and he wrote to her and told her how much we missed her and how he hoped we could put the past behind us and finally make amends. After six months of silence, he at last received a reply, which is when Mum told me what they'd done and that Jennifer was living in Scotland, with two beautiful dogs as her new 'babies'.

It was a wonderful day when my whole family was finally reunited and we were able to put all the family demons behind us. I'm so pleased to have my big sister back and, although she lives so far away and I don't often see her, my love for her will always remain as strong as ever. Whenever I'm feeling sad, I know now that she's just a phone call or text message away, with her many wise words and the ability always to put a smile on my face.

Two years ago, the reuniting of our family was finally completed when I was walking along the road in Horsham and bumped into my cousin Jessica. We just stopped and looked at each other, and, although we hadn't had any contact for years, we recognised each other straightaway. She has a beautiful little boy and girl now, and meeting her again was a wonderful moment. Since then, Uncle Ray and Dad have also made contact again, so thankfully all the old wounds have now been healed.

But things weren't getting any better in other areas of my life. When I was coming up for my sixteenth birthday, a friend of mine (the girl who'd introduced me to inhaling aerosols) suggested I throw a party at my house, which, she assured me, would stop people picking on me and help me to make friends with some of the local kids. I was very low by this time and it was a very scary idea for lots of reasons, not least because I knew there was a chance I'd arrange it all and then have to cancel it if I had a bad panic attack. But, as we were about to sell the house in Burstow, I eventually allowed myself to be persuaded to hold what I saw as a sort of 'goodbye party' to the place that had been my home for the previous 16 years.

When I told my mum one evening that I was going over to my friend's house, she was really pleased, because it was the first time I'd tried to go out since my experience in the nightclub when a girl had broken a glass in my face. My friend and I waited until it was dark and then went into town and scattered flyers – with my address on them – all over the place. I can see now that it was a recipe for disaster, but at the time I was extremely vulnerable and desperate to do something that would put an end to the dreadful fear I felt whenever I thought about leaving my room.

On 22 July, I woke up feeling really nervous. I spent six hours getting ready, trying to disguise my face and putting on the most outrageous outfit – a long, luminous-green mac with purple flares, a purple top and green shoes. As usual, I thought that if people focused on what I was wearing, it would draw their attention away from my face.

When I'd told my family about the party, they'd been really

pleased that I'd decided to do something social. My dad and brothers decorated our huge garage with lights and a jungle theme and my mum put on a wonderful spread of food and made a really good non-alcoholic punch. I nearly cried when I came downstairs and saw what they'd done and all the effort they'd made for me.

Before people started to arrive, I went to Fay's grave and asked her to be with me at the party. Although I was really scared, I felt I'd have the strength to go through with it all if she were by my side.

I'm sure everyone who's ever had a party has had that feeling that no one's going to come, so I was very relieved when people started to arrive at about 8.30. Dad had roped off the garden and garage area so that the party stayed outside and away from the house, but my family had no idea that I'd invited totally random people by throwing out flyers all over Crawley.

By about 10pm, the place was absolutely packed and I finally plucked up the courage to leave my room. As I walked into the garage, I could hear people whispering and sneering at me and not one single person said, 'Happy birthday.' There was food everywhere, the punch had been poured out and replaced by alcohol and there was a group of boys at the back of the garage smoking drugs. It felt as though they'd all just come to destroy me. I was too scared to say anything, but I couldn't go back into the house because I didn't want my mum and dad to see my reaction and know something was wrong. So instead I started drinking a bottle of vodka that someone had brought, hoping it would calm my nerves and enable me to shut out what was going on around me.

But eventually it was all too much and I escaped to the churchyard and just sat by Fay's grave, wishing she was with me and that the party would end and all those people, who didn't even like me, let alone care about me, would go home.

Then suddenly I heard shouting; I could see two boys fighting in the road and smell smoke coming from the garage. My heart started racing and I felt really panicky. Everything was getting out of control and it was completely the opposite of what I'd hoped, very naively, it would all be like. And then everything went silent.

After a few moments I plucked up the courage to look through the bushes and could see my father and brothers throwing everyone out. It turned out that some of the boys had snuck into the house and stolen all the alcohol they could find, one of them had tried to hit my brother and then my dad had caught someone setting fire to the garage.

Although I was really upset, I was also hugely relieved that it was all over. My dad and brothers were furious with me for inviting such awful people, but my mum just hugged me and took me upstairs to my room, where someone had left me my one and only present – a pile of poo in my bathroom.

It was a horrible experience and I just couldn't understand why everyone was so intent on showing such disrespect to me and to my family. It was obviously very foolish to have set about things in the way I did, but it did confirm one thing to me: there was absolutely no chance that I would ever be accepted by the young people of Crawley.

I was very frightened at the prospect of moving out of the old manor house in Burstow. It had been my home all my life and was the one place where I felt relatively safe, despite my ghostly experiences there and the constant fear of the huge spiders that graciously allowed us to live with them. But, when the time came, I packed all my belongings and carefully labelled my boxes, including the four that were completely full of my essential make-up.

On the day we moved, Dad was very snappy and obviously upset, which wasn't really surprising because he was selling everything he'd worked so hard for. But my brothers had all left home by this time, Dad was becoming increasingly busy with work and because we hadn't taken on any more help in the house since the fire, Mum was doing all the cleaning herself and a large house with 11 bedrooms was just too much for her to maintain.

Although I didn't know at the time, my parents had also decided to make the move because they felt that living in such a secluded place in the country was making it all too easy for me to hide myself away from the rest of the world. They thought that moving closer to Crawley might encourage me to leave my bedroom from time to time, particularly as it would mean that, if I did venture out into town, I'd be close enough to get home quickly if I had a panic attack.

However, it turned out that there was more to Dad's grumpiness that day than we realised, and by the time we moved into the new house he was very ill. He'd already lost a huge amount of weight and when he began throwing up green fluid, Mum called the hospital. They confirmed her suspicion that Dad had very severe food poisoning – which he'd got from a meat pie he'd bought locally during the move – and said he needed to rest. So for the next couple of weeks he was shut away in their new bedroom, unable to do anything.

As I started to unpack my boxes in the new house, I couldn't find any of the ones labelled 'Make-up' and became increasingly panicked as Mum and I searched again and again without success. Finally having to accept that they simply weren't there, I then found out from my brother that Dad had thrown them all on the bonfire, thinking that by doing so he'd be helping me. I was devastated; my head was spinning and I felt physically sick.

Luckily I always carried a huge bag of make-up with me everywhere I went, so I still had my absolute essentials, but the things that had been burned were my supplies, including my hairdryer, hair products and so on. It was as though someone had taken away my mask and thrown that on the fire, leaving me exposed and vulnerable. I hated Dad for doing that to me and wanted to scream at him, so it was even more frustrating not to be able to confront him because he was so ill.

In a state of complete panic, I locked myself in my new bedroom and smashed everything up, and when I came out again, my wrists were dripping with blood, my eyes were swollen up like golf balls and I'd tried to strangle myself with one of my dad's ties. When I finally calmed down, I wrote a two-page list of all the things I needed and begged Mum to go to the shops to buy them. She was extremely busy unpacking, but when she saw the state I was in she just hugged me and assured me she'd replace it all. She was also angry with my dad, although I now realise he was only trying to help me. But you can't help BDD sufferers by doing something so drastic; they need to be given time to adapt to any changes very slowly, and the fact that I had just had to move to a new house was bad enough without discovering my make-up and hair products had all been destroyed.

Dad was ill for a fortnight. I think it must have been stress related too, because he wasn't himself during the move. Looking back on it, I hate the fact that I was so concerned about something so superficial when the food poisoning could have killed him, and, although I couldn't help it at the time, I very much regret that I didn't concentrate on looking after him instead.

9

Numbing the Pain

Trying to kill myself became quite a regular occurrence. Some attempts would be more serious than others, depending on how many tablets I could get my hands on, but they were all serious attempts, and I made sure no one knew what I was doing. I'd wait until everyone was out and then go round the house and take whatever I could find – paracetamol, cold tablets, whatever there happened to be – and if there was a whole pack, I'd take them all. Eventually Mum started locking all the tablets away, but it didn't matter where she hid them, because I'd destroy everything until I found them.

Immediately after taking the tablets I'd lie down on my bed feeling completely calm and try to go to sleep, thinking, 'Hopefully I won't wake up tomorrow, and then everything will be OK.' So, in a crazy way, it did have a bit of a calming effect on me, although when I woke up after each attempt I'd be very sick and feel really weak and shaky. I'd pinch myself in the hope of finding I wasn't really still there, and then I'd feel even worse, and really angry with myself for being such a failure. Fay had died in an accident and I was taking overdoses and *trying* to kill myself, but, however many tablets I took, I didn't die.

The normal pattern was for my suicide attempts to follow a day when I'd been self-harming, feeling angry and slashing cuts on my wrists with a razor. I'm very lucky to have only quite small scars now, as I didn't usually cut very deeply, although I do have a couple of more obvious ones where I stuck a pair of scissors into my arm. But I wasn't trying to kill myself by cutting my wrists and arms because I knew that, if I cut a main artery, all the blood would spurt out, and that wasn't the way I wanted to go. It was just a way of releasing some of the pain. The physical pain took the mental pain away and calmed me down, for a while at least.

I had bulimia at this stage and, although I didn't think what I was doing was strange in any way, I'd go for weeks without eating and then suddenly want to binge. I wouldn't care what I ate, I just wanted to eat, and then I'd have to be sick afterwards.

I was often alone in the house because Mum was working nearby in a surveyors' office, but she'd ring me during the day to make sure I was all right; we had a code so that I'd know it was her and answer the phone. Apparently, on one particular day she rang and didn't get an answer, so as soon as she could she came home. When she walked into the kitchen she was confronted by absolute chaos – food and mess everywhere.

I'd gathered together every ingredient I could find in the fridge and made a huge pizza in a deep baking tin. Obviously you can't make a pizza with inches of topping on it, and when I put it in the oven it didn't cook. So I'd scooped out all this disgusting topping and left a huge mess everywhere, thinking I'd have a chance to clear it all up before Mum came home in the evening.

When Mum saw all the chaos in the kitchen, she went upstairs to look for me in the bathroom and found sick everywhere. By this time she was feeling very anxious and went round the whole house searching for me and then into the garden, where she could hear me sobbing in the shed. She was really confused about what was going on, but rather than force a confrontation, and to give herself time to think it over, she decided not to let me know she was there and simply went back to work. Later she had a go at me about the mess in the kitchen but didn't say she'd heard me crying, because she didn't want to embarrass me. In fact, when she did finally confront me some time later about what had happened that day, I was so embarrassed I took an overdose.

After that it became a nightmare, because everyone in the house knew what had happened and realised I had an eating disorder. If I was forced to eat something and then went to the toilet, Dad would tell someone to see where I'd gone. So they'd come upstairs and stand outside the bathroom door, and I'd have to turn on the tap to hide the sound of my being sick. If I knew I wouldn't be able to be sick, I wouldn't eat anything, and I'd hide my food in a napkin and throw it down the toilet.

All I'd have during the day would be a cup of coffee and then a slice of toast for dinner, with lots of water in between; then the next day I'd eat a whole box of chocolates, have an absolute binge and be sick. So, it was really anorexia and bulimia both rolled into one, which I think is often the case.

Inevitably I became very thin – although I never felt thin – and got down to six stone, which is a shocking weight for someone of my height. I had to wear children's clothes because nothing else would fit me, and my nails were like paper – you could just flick them off as they grew. I slept almost all the time because I felt so weak, so I wasn't able to do anything and certainly couldn't have worked. When I was asleep I'd dream that I was eating or that I'd been to McDonald's, so in my mind it was true and when I woke up I'd tell myself, 'Well, that's OK. I've had something to eat.' I'd fantasise about food and almost hallucinate about eating.

I love food now, and I eat loads, but I still suffer from irritable bowel syndrome and get a lot of stomach aches, which isn't surprising with all the messing about my stomach's had to cope with. I can't take paracetamol any more because I took so many during those years, and even just a couple make my stomach really hurt. I've since read that taking an overdose of paracetamol can cause paralysis and liver failure – among other things – but I didn't know that at the time. All I knew was that I wanted to die.

Mum found me after one of my early serious suicide attempts and gave me salt water to make me vomit. I'd had a panic attack and had taken all the tablets I could lay my hands on, and I remember waking up with Mum screaming, 'Racheal, what have you done?' The next day I was very weak and sick, but I refused to go to hospital. The trouble was that trying to get me out of the house at all when I was so ill was difficult enough, so there was no chance of my leaving my room when I'd taken an overdose and looked really awful. But it wasn't just a case of saying, 'I'm not going.' I'd be trying to strangle myself or beat myself up, so it was impossible for Mum to force me to go. In fact, I think I did go to hospital on one occasion and they gave me something to make me sick, but I made so many attempts to kill myself that I can't really separate one from another now.

Another time, when I was 16, I took a massive overdose of paracetamol washed down with vodka. I became very dozy and started frothing at the mouth and being sick. A friend came over, and although she knew what I'd done, she wasn't mentally very well herself, so she didn't think to get any help for me. She was a very depressed girl too, and suffered from agoraphobia, so she could understand how I was feeling and would come over to my house and talk to me through the bedroom door. She also took an overdose later which I think may have been a cry for help, because she phoned me sobbing and told me what she'd done and I rang for an ambulance. I forced myself to leave my room to visit her in hospital, and when I saw her lying there looking so ill and skinny, I was really afraid in case I was influencing her by my own behaviour. And it was then that I realised just how serious it was and that I had to stop.

What also eventually helped to put me off doing that to myself was reading a story in a magazine about a girl who'd taken an overdose and lost the use of her legs. Although I didn't care if I died, I'd never realised I might become disabled instead, and thinking about what would happen to me if I suddenly lost the use of my limbs was another incentive to stop.

I don't know how I'm still alive, and when I think about it now I wonder what I was doing. But at the time I had no idea there was anything strange about my behaviour.

10

A Ray of Hope

It was really disappointing when the counselling didn't work out, as there didn't seem to be anywhere else for us to turn for help. By the time I was 16, I'd already spent the better part of three years locked in my room, angry and hating myself, afraid to come out and be seen, and facing a bleak and miserable future I didn't dare think about.

Then one day when Mum was watching television there was a message at the end of a programme that said something like, 'Do you know anybody who thinks they're hideously ugly?' – and then it pretty much listed my symptoms. Mum was desperate by this time and prepared to try anything that might lead to getting some help for me. I don't think she could really believe what she was hearing, but she immediately rushed to ring the phone number they'd given and said, 'I think my daughter is suffering from all the symptoms you mentioned.'

They were looking for people to take part in a GMTV programme called *The Time, The Place*, and after talking to Mum they told her they'd like me to appear on it. For someone for whom leaving the house varied from being very hard to absolutely impossible, and who wouldn't even let her own family see her without her face covered in some sort of camouflage, it was hardly surprising I refused. Just the thought of trying to face the general public on television made me feel physically sick, and it was simply out of the question.

So, when Mum first told me about it I went absolutely mad. But she was insistent and wouldn't leave me alone, and eventually asked someone from the show to speak to me on the phone. They begged me to take part and said, 'There are a lot of people who feel the same way as you do and, if you can be brave enough to speak up, you might be able to get some help.'

It was the first time any of us had heard that there were other people with a similar problem, which I think was what made Mum so determined to pursue it. It must have been really hard for her to watch me deteriorate, both physically and mentally, over the years, and I know she was constantly searching for *anything* that might result in my being given some sort of treatment.

The people I spoke to on the phone were really nice and they told me that there was going to be a doctor on the show who might be able to find out what was wrong with me. But that didn't really help much, because I didn't see myself as being ill. Just as with so many other similar types of illness, the hardest thing is to admit that there's anything wrong in the first place. So I suppose there was that fear as well: as much as I wanted to get help, and however tempted I was by the chance of discovering I wasn't alone, I was afraid of having to face the possibility that I was a bit crazy. Also, doing the programme would be a contradiction of everything I did in my everyday life: it would mean going straight from hiding myself away in my room to appearing on national television, and I was appalled at the prospect of admitting to the world that I cut myself and of talking about all the things that were so private to me. People who take

an overdose are either crying out for help or just want to die –
and I fitted into the second category. The things I did were very
much *not* for attention, and no one else knew I did them.

So I really, really didn't want to do the programme. But, having
tried to persuade me, Mum changed her tactics and simply
insisted, and the whole thing triggered some very severe panic
attacks. The night before the programme I was screaming and
crying and smashing things, while Dad was going mad at Mum,
shouting, 'Leave her alone. What are you doing to her? She
doesn't want to do it.' He could see the effect it was having on
me and was obviously very distressed by it, but Mum's response
was, 'She's got to face it. I've *got* to do this. We *have* to find out
what's wrong with her.' She was absolutely determined, despite
opposition from everyone else in the family, because by this time
she was prepared to do almost anything, and to take almost any
risk, if there was even the slightest chance it might lead to me
getting some help. I was always having panic attacks anyway, and
I think she thought, 'Just one big panic attack and then we might
be able to make her better.'

So, not only was I carrying on like a crazy person, but Mum
and Dad were arguing as well. Mum was like a person possessed
and refused to leave me alone. Sobbing and shouting, I locked
myself in my bedroom, but she just kept insisting, 'You *are* going
to do this programme. You *have* to do it.' She'd finally been offered
a tiny ray of hope that we might be able to find out what was
wrong with me, and I think she'd have done anything rather than
let the opportunity slip away.

No mother would be able to bear seeing her daughter hiding
herself away in her room and trying to kill herself because she
believes she's different. So, although Mum's tactics were extreme,
they were born of desperation. But getting me on to the
programme was quite another story, and she quite literally had to
drag me on to it.

The night before, I was self-harming, cutting myself and saying, 'If you make me go on this programme, I'll kill myself. I'm not going to wake up in the morning. I'm not going to do it.' It was probably the worst attack I'd ever had, but I suppose Mum just thought, 'She's already tried to kill herself, so how much worse can it get?'

We'd seen a counsellor and that hadn't worked, and there didn't seem to be anyone else who could help, so it was a case of pushing me in at the deep end and hoping I'd swim. Obviously at the time I didn't understand all this; I just thought she was trying to force me to do something I didn't want to do and I was really upset that she was being so cruel to me. But I wonder where I'd be now if she hadn't persisted and hadn't held out against everyone else who was telling her to leave me alone.

Because of the illness, I did tend to blame my mum for a lot of things. I'd get angry with her and ask her why she'd brought me into the world. Because I was born with the umbilical cord wrapped three times around my neck, I used to say that I'd tried to kill myself on the way out, and that it was a sign I shouldn't be here. It must have been very upsetting for Mum and I feel really guilty about it all now, although I think she understands.

One of my worst anxieties about doing the programme was the possibility that my make-up wouldn't go right. If it didn't, I knew I wouldn't be going anywhere, and then what was I going to do? It would be really embarrassing to have to wear my Muslim veil for the whole world to see. Mum said she'd buy me some clothes, but that doesn't work with BDD sufferers. You could spend a million pounds on them and they're still not going to go out if they don't want to.

The programme's producers tried to make it as easy as possible for me and in the end it was all arranged on a sort of 'see how you feel' basis. When a car and a producer arrived in the morning to take us to the television studio, I was having a terrible panic attack and refusing to go, so Mum had to drag me out of the house and force me into the car. Some people might say that was wrong, but it wasn't. What was she meant to do? She'd tried everything else and I wasn't making any progress, and she'd simply run out of options.

The programme dealt with various extreme appearance-related issues, and the fact that there were other people on it who felt the same as I did was comforting in itself. There were a couple of people with BDD and one person who'd tried to give herself liposuction by cutting the fat out of her legs. When you hear things like that, you look at the people and think, 'Why are they doing that to themselves?' – and then you look at yourself. It's quite a shock to the system. Although I could relate to what they'd done and understand how they felt – I thought *my* legs were fat and had tried to cut them on several occasions – there was nothing wrong with these people.

At that time my hair was permed and was long and thick and hung like a curtain over my face, so throughout the entire programme you couldn't see my face at all. I felt really uncomfortable the whole time and hardly said anything, so Mum did most of the talking.

I do remember that someone said to me, 'You look lovely,' and I said, 'Please don't say that.' I can't describe what it was like when someone complimented me. It was as though they'd said something bad and I couldn't take it in. When someone bullied me I'd just take it because, even though it really hurt, I felt I deserved whatever they were saying because I hated myself so much. I'd just think, 'Fine. You call me what you want, because I know it already.' That's why I started making myself look bizarre: I was getting the punishment I deserved. The comments people made about the way I had made myself look didn't really hurt me directly, but if someone said, 'Oh, you're really pretty,' it made me feel sick. Why were they lying to me? Why couldn't they just face the truth and help me to face it?

There was an American doctor on the show, and after hearing what Mum said he told her, 'Your daughter is suffering from an illness called body dysmorphic disorder.'

Although it sounds a strange thing to say, I think she could have cried with joy. We'd never even heard of BDD before; we didn't know it existed, and in fact very little was known about it anywhere at that time. There was a bit of research being done into it in America, but almost nothing in the UK. But for Mum just to hear that there was some sort of diagnosis was fantastic. If I had a recognised illness, there might be a cure, and it meant that I wasn't simply crazy – which I think she'd known all along.

Of course, I didn't think I was ill at all. I just felt as though I was cursed and that I didn't deserve to have a life. Why did I deserve to enjoy myself when Fay couldn't? It was really depressing to think, 'This is me. This is what I've grown up to be. I don't want to face the world. I don't want to do anything with my life. I just want to hide away in my room for ever.'

I was always asking Mum and Dad to let me have plastic surgery, to get myself 'fixed', because when I looked in the mirror I saw a completely disfigured person, and I was convinced everyone was laughing at me. I knew there were a lot of very brave people with terrible disfigurements, from burns and other injuries, who faced the world every day. I've always admired people who overcome disabilities, and it used to make me even angrier with myself when I looked at people with illnesses and thought, 'Why is it they can face the world and be OK and I can't? Why am I so selfish? When I don't judge anybody else on the basis of what they look like, why am I so concerned about what people are going to think of me?'

When I went on *The Time, The Place*, it was the first time I'd faced my fear, and after the show, as I listened to the doctor explaining what BDD was, it was also the first time I'd faced the possibility that what I was seeing when I looked in the mirror might be an illusion, although the idea took a very long time to sink in. It's really quite shocking when you're diagnosed as suffering from an illness and you suddenly have to face the possibility that everything you thought you were, everything you've always been, hasn't actually been you at all. I think if it had been a case of having to accept that I was physically disfigured, I could have learned to deal with that. But it was all the other aspects of BDD that made it so difficult to cope with.

Paradoxically, my immediate feeling was that it was nice to know I was suffering from an illness, because it meant that all my panic attacks weren't just part of 'me'. But I couldn't really believe it, and to begin with I thought, 'No, I'm just awful.' I'd spent so long believing I was a horrible person that I couldn't really absorb the idea that I might be ill rather than having the terrible character flaws I'd got so used to hating in myself. So, although it was comforting to know there was a name for what I was suffering from, it didn't fundamentally change how I felt.

As Dad hadn't agreed with Mum making me do the programme, he didn't come with us to the television studio, but he did record it on video, which in retrospect was a mistake. Although I'd felt a bit better after talking to the doctor, all hell broke loose again when I watched the video footage. I was absolutely horrified and was screaming and crying and going mad at Mum, saying, 'How could you let me go on national TV and let everyone see me? How could you let that happen?'

I was so distraught that my dad blamed Mum even more. He went absolutely nuts and was shouting, 'Don't do this to her.' In fact, I think my dad has definitely got something wrong himself, although to a much lesser degree, and he understood how hard it was for me. But obviously Mum wanted me to go on TV in the hope that it would somehow 'cure' me, or at least lead to us finding out what was wrong with me.

After I'd watched the show at home, I got hold of a bottle of vodka and a load of paracetamol, locked myself in my bedroom and took the lot. I could still hear my parents arguing with each other, my dad shouting, 'Why are you making her do this? Just leave her alone!' and Mum saying, 'If we don't find out what's wrong with her, she's going to kill herself. You don't understand. There's no other way we can help her.'

I didn't understand at the time why Mum had made me do it, although I do now. Part of the problem was that when I was younger she used to send me to ballet lessons, tap-dancing lessons, acting classes and auditions for TV programmes and plays. In fact, she sent me to one audition that was really quite funny – in retrospect. It was for the title role in a stage production of *Annie*. As you'd expect, all the other kids at this audition had red hair, and they were all really confident, singing and dancing around the place. But when the organisers came to me and said, 'Hi! What's your name?' I kept my head down and muttered, 'Racheal' in a timid little voice. It would have been hard to imagine anyone less appropriate for the part than me.

Mum had her first child at 17 – a boy, followed by two more boys – and she'd missed out on so much herself that when she eventually had a little girl she wanted me to be able to do all the things she didn't get to do. I think she was trying to make me come out of my shell, and to raise my confidence level. But I was a very shy, nervous little girl and I was never going to be as confident as Mum was, so it had the opposite effect. On the other hand, maybe the BDD was already there, and maybe I was even more insecure than a normal shy child, which is why it didn't work.

So, when Mum was trying to make me do the television programme, I thought it was for the same reasons: I thought she wanted to push me out there in front of the media and let me be seen. But I wasn't interested in that, and never have been, and I felt deeply embarrassed that people had seen me. Looking back on it now, though, I realise she was just desperately trying to get help for me.

When I woke up the next morning, having taken all the tablets and drunk loads of vodka, I felt really depressed, and I begged my parents again to let me have surgery. In fact, I still cringe now when I watch my past self, and it sometimes makes me quite tearful, not so much because of what I look like, but more because of my body language.

When I watched the video of *The Time, The Place*, I couldn't believe it. I was shaking violently throughout the whole programme, peering out from underneath the curtain of hair that was hanging over my face, and looking desperately sad. I think that was what made me realise that the way I was behaving just wasn't normal. I thought I looked terrible, a complete freak, and the panic attack it triggered was partly because I hated what I looked like and partly because I realised how self-obsessed I must have appeared to other people. Seeing the girl who used to be 'Miss I'm-Never-Going-to-Care-About-What-I-Look-Like' shaking and being unable to look anyone in the eye was a huge shock and made me really angry with myself and determined I was never going to do anything like that again.

So, although I suppose the immediate result was that Mum felt more optimistic because we had a diagnosis of what was wrong with me, the effect on me was more or less to put me right back where I'd started. When I later went on to do more TV programmes, Dad eventually stopped recording them, pretending he'd forgotten, because my disappointment was easier to deal with than my absolute distress when I watched myself.

But then, about two weeks after the show, the letters started coming in – big packets of them forwarded from the television company. I think I received about 250 letters from people who'd seen the programme and felt just like I did, and I began to realise I wasn't alone. They were from all sorts of people, and quite a few of them sent me photographs – photographs of lovely, beautiful people with no signs of the disfigurements and physical horrors they said they had. And it was then that the first glimmer of light began to dawn: maybe what the doctor had said was true. Maybe I was suffering from an illness and the person I saw looking back at me in the mirror was not real at all, but only in my mind. If that were true, then perhaps I could slowly come to accept that everything I'd thought for years constituted 'me' wasn't actually 'me' at all – and that was the very first step on the long and often rocky road to recovery.

The fact that there were other people who felt just like I did was an extraordinary piece of information to absorb, and, although part of me still didn't really believe I was suffering from an illness, another part of me felt an enormous relief, as though a huge weight had been lifted from my shoulders. It seems strange to say that, as most people would be horrified to find out they had an illness, but for me it was like a reprieve.

With BDD it's not just a case of hating yourself on the outside – you hate who you've become – and I *really* hated myself. Hiding myself away because of what I looked like didn't make sense to me; it contradicted all my beliefs. I can say with my hand on my heart that I never judge people on what they look like, so I was angry with myself for being so concerned about what other people would think of me. I've since learned that I don't have time for anyone who judges me on my appearance – that's their problem, not mine; it doesn't make *me* a bad person. But back then I didn't understand that.

For the first time in my life I started to feel good about myself; I realised that, no matter how ill I was, I could do something worthwhile and help people, and that made me feel as though the pain I went through every single day might be worthwhile.

I started writing back to all the people who'd written to me, and that was the beginning of an exchange of letters that really helped me. It was the first time I'd had a dialogue with people who weren't just reassuring me, and it was like a therapy, allowing me to start to release some of the pain that had been bottled up inside me for so long.

A lot of my anger was the result of everyone trying to make me feel better by assuring me I wasn't 'ugly'. But to me that just felt as though they were belittling my concerns. Although I still find compliments very hard to take, I can overcome my discomfort enough to say 'Thank you'. But back then I just wanted to say, 'Look, I know what I am. Don't patronise me. Just listen to me.'

Then suddenly, after the programme, I was writing to people and telling them how I felt, and they were writing back to me and saying they felt the same. We weren't trying to give each other confidence or reassurance, which simply doesn't work for people with BDD. All they want is someone to understand how they're feeling so that they don't feel quite so crazy. Also, it was a new experience for me to think that at least some people wouldn't look at me and think, 'Oh, she's just vain,' because I realise that some of the symptoms of BDD can come across like that. If you say to people, 'I'm not coming out because I don't look right,' they can't help but think, 'Why is she so preoccupied with her appearance?' But the reality of how it makes you feel is so much more than that. So it was really nice being able to communicate with other people with similar experiences.

Gradually I began to realise that forcing myself to be brave and to do things I didn't want to do could help other people, and it was that knowledge that helped me even more than knowing what was wrong with me. Realising I could do something 'good' made me feel that perhaps my life wasn't a total waste of time; maybe it had a purpose after all. Having always asked myself the same questions – Why am I here? What's the point? – it finally seemed possible that I'd found the answers.

Although I'd never have admitted it at the time, if Mum hadn't made me go on that programme I don't think I'd ever have started to get better. It might have been easier if I'd been able to say to a doctor, 'Look, these are my symptoms. What's wrong with me?' Having to go on national television to get help certainly wasn't the way I'd have chosen, but perhaps the end justifies the means. At the time, I was really angry with Mum for making me do it, and even now I feel angry with her when I think about it, which is crazy because it did so much good. But I always felt I was forced to do it, because, when the producer came to our house and sat outside my bedroom door I couldn't be rude, and I didn't know what else to do.

The producers must have been desperate to find someone to appear on the programme – obviously it's really hard to get a BDD sufferer to talk about their illness – so they had to be very careful how they approached me. I suppose the fact that they ended up having to send a car and a producer to try to coax me out of my room was good in a way, because it made it clear just how serious the illness is. It showed the production people that it wasn't something they could glorify on TV; it was something they had to tread very carefully with.

After that, Mum started trying to find out anything she could about BDD, but there was very little information available. She eventually found a book called *The Broken Mirror: Understanding and Treating Body Dysmorphic Disorder*, written by an American doctor called Dr Katharine Phillips, which she read from cover to cover. It was obvious I had all the symptoms it described, which was comforting in a strange way, particularly for Mum, because it confirmed the diagnosis we'd been given. It was quite a short book at the time, but the new edition, which was published in 2005 by Oxford University Press, is much longer, which shows how much more is known about BDD today – at least in America – although even now relatively few people have heard of it.

You don't suddenly get better when you've been ill for so long, particularly with something like BDD. But, although that first step was a really hard step to take, I dread to think what would have happened to me if I hadn't been forced into taking it.

11

Small Steps

After I'd been on *The Time, The Place*, the newspapers started ringing up, because it was the first time most people had ever heard of BDD. The *Daily Mail* wanted to do a piece on me, but my reaction was pretty much the same as with the TV programme and I really didn't want to do it. Mum told them to come down anyway, but when they arrived I went mad and refused to come out of my room. I embarrassed her completely and must have come across as very rude to the people from the newspaper, but I just couldn't do it.

They'd brought a make-up artist with them because they wanted to take a picture, and they tried to reassure me by saying, 'Don't worry, we'll make you look OK.' But the last thing I wanted was someone else doing my make-up; it had to be done a certain way and even I couldn't get it right on most days. The reporter was lovely, but I don't think she realised just how ill I was until she had to deal with me. It was only after she'd sat outside my bedroom door begging me to come out that I think she understood I wasn't somebody who wanted fame.

Eventually they had to leave without their interview, but they came back another day and again the reporter sat outside my bedroom door begging me to come out. It seemed really rude to ignore her, particularly when she'd had to leave empty-handed last time, and that made me feel even worse. She was saying, 'We need to get this disorder noticed, Racheal. You're the only person who can speak about it. You're so brave. Please let us do the story,' which really made me want to try. She finally managed to persuade me by talking about how much good I could do if I helped get coverage for BDD. I'd had such a good response to the television programme that I knew she was right, and I really wanted to force myself to do it.

So I agreed to do the interview and to have my picture taken, although again I blamed my mum for making me do it. Today if I said, 'Go away,' they'd have to listen to me rather than take any notice of what my mum said, but when you're 16 your parents have a certain amount of control over situations like that.

When the story appeared in the paper, I became really ill again, which is the way it always went. The article was about BDD and was really good; they did a brilliant write-up, although they called it 'the ugliness syndrome' and 'ugly' is a word I really don't like. But when the newspaper arrived I immediately looked at the photograph and felt physically sick. They'd done their best with it – particularly considering all they'd had to go through with me to get it – but the truth was that there was no photograph anyone could have taken that I'd have been happy with. I started crying and screaming at Mum, 'I'm never doing this again. Leave me alone. Stop making me do it. I can't do it any more,' and then I went upstairs and made cuts all over my wrists. I remained ill until the letters started to come in and I began to think that I might have done some good after all. But, although it was nice to feel I was helping people, the negative side was that I began to be more focused on my looks.

After the article appeared in the *Daily Mail*, someone from the *Daily Star* rang up and asked me to do an interview and let them take some photos. 'It won't be anything awful,' they assured me. 'You can wear a bikini.'

It was like some sort of joke. I couldn't even have worn a bikini on the beach, so the thought of appearing in one in the newspaper made me feel almost hysterical with anxiety. I already felt hideous, like some sort of freak show, and I knew I wasn't the sort of girl they'd want as a model for their newspaper, so it felt as though they were just trying to exploit me by saying, 'Ha ha, look at her. She says she thinks she's ugly, but look at her now, modelling in the paper.' I felt really offended and insulted and was convinced they just wanted to make a laughing stock of me.

When the doctor who'd diagnosed me on *The Time, The Place* talked to us after the show, he told Mum about a clinic in London where they might be able to help me, and then it was left up to us to try to get the help I needed. So, after I'd done the *Daily Mail* interview, Mum took me to see a doctor at the Priory Clinic, who appeared to be the only doctor in the UK who knew anything about BDD at the time. I think he was mainly involved with treating people with obsessive-compulsive disorder (OCD), but I suppose there's a link between the two, as there can be aspects of OCD in BDD.

The prospect of talking to a doctor was very hard for me to deal with, but at the same time I was excited because I felt it was my only real chance of getting better. I could hardly believe that finally I was going to be able to talk to someone who would understand what I was going through and who was in a position to help me.

Knowing that there were other people suffering from the same illness had been the first step towards starting to feel less of a freak. Both receiving the letters that had been written in response to the television programme and newspaper article and writing back to people had given me an enormous amount of comfort. I could see from the photographs people sent me that, whatever they thought about their physical appearance, the truth was that they looked perfectly all right. So, it had begun to dawn on me that, if that was true of other people, maybe what I was seeing when I looked in the mirror wasn't there either. It's like someone showing you their hand and telling you how much they hate the awful wart on it, but when you look there's nothing there.

However, although that first glimmer of understanding and the feeling of having helped other people had started to make me feel as though there might be something to live for after all, going to see a BDD specialist would be on quite a different level. It had taken a long time to sink in, but I'd begun to realise I had an illness. So, although the prospect of talking to a doctor filled me with panic, it was also the first time I'd had any feeling of hope for the future. It was a really difficult step for me to take, but I kept reminding myself that it might lead to a cure and was perhaps my one chance to have a more normal life.

I sat in the waiting room at the Priory Clinic with my mum, feeling both nervous and excited. Eventually my name was called, but, as we both stood up, Mum was told quite brusquely that she couldn't come in with me. I began to panic, but I'd come so far I knew I had to see it through.

I was uncomfortable from the moment I met the doctor. The completely incomprehensible medical terms he used left me feeling inadequate and stupid, and he didn't seem to make any attempt to find out if I understood what he was saying. Then, as I started to explain to him how I had to hide my face behind a mask of make-up or a Muslim-type veil before I could even be seen by my own family, he laughed. I suppose it probably does sound funny to other people, but amusement wasn't at all the reaction I'd expected from a doctor and I felt deeply ashamed and embarrassed. One of the problems with BDD is that you feel everyone's laughing at you anyway, even if they're not, so if someone actually does, it has a really bad effect.

Although mortified and humiliated, I managed to continue with the consultation, but it felt increasingly like a BDD question-and-answer session rather than an opportunity for me to talk about my problems openly with someone who understood them. The questions the doctor asked me seemed to be directed at eliciting information about BDD in general, rather than finding out how the illness affected me personally. I know that BDD distorts your perception of reality, but, even allowing for that, I felt more like a guinea-pig than someone who was being offered sympathetic help.

After the consultation, I was given the option of being admitted into the hospital at the clinic for therapy, which sounded as though it would consist primarily of having all mirrors removed and being encouraged to 'pull myself together'. One aspect of BDD is that you either look in the mirror all the time or you avoid mirrors at all costs, and I was someone who looked in the mirror 24/7. Even now, I have to stop myself from doing it, because I know that, if you stare at anything long enough, you're sure to discover its flaws. So, taking all the mirrors away from someone with BDD doesn't sound like rocket science, although I was very frightened by the idea. Maybe if I'd felt comfortable with the doctor, I'd have been more able to consider putting myself in his hands and doing whatever he thought would be effective. But it's very difficult for people with BDD to trust anyone they don't know very well, and unfortunately I didn't feel comfortable with him.

Being admitted to the clinic would also have been expensive; I think the consultation alone cost £150, and that was about ten years ago. Although I know my parents would have spent any amount of money to help me get better, under the circumstances it was a cost that didn't seem to be justified.

I've always been quite sensitive to how other people are feeling, and, even when my illness was at its most severe, I could pick up on their emotions. So I did feel that my instincts about the doctor were justified, even allowing for my probably distorted viewpoint at the time.

Most people still know little or nothing about BDD, but even less was known about it at that time. With one exception, every doctor on every television or radio programme I've ever been on has asked me questions about the illness beforehand. The only one who didn't was Dr Linda Papadopoulos, the psychologist who used to be on ITV's *This Morning* and the first series of *Big Brother*. I didn't have to tell her anything at all; she completely analysed me and understood everything, and was also very warm and friendly and made me feel comfortable by the way she treated me. So it wasn't simply that I felt uncomfortable talking to people about my illness — although in most cases that was true — because I was happy to talk to Dr Papadopoulos. So I'm sure my perception of the attitude of the doctor at the clinic wasn't completely imagined. I was convinced he didn't understand me or empathise with me at all.

One of the biggest fears BDD sufferers have is that people are going to judge them and look down on them. So the last thing they want is to be faced with someone who's hyper-intelligent, talking in medical language they can't understand and confirming their feeling that their behaviour is strange and there's something wrong with them. People suffering from illnesses like BDD and OCD are very vulnerable and it's essential that anyone who deals with them has compassion and is able to relate to their emotions and not make them feel they're being coldly analysed or criticised.

That same doctor is apparently now one of England's leading experts on BDD, so obviously some people find him helpful. But I do wonder if perhaps to some extent they're actually helping themselves by accepting they have a problem and taking that first step on the road to their recovery.

All I can say is that he didn't help me and I was left feeling that, after all my excitement about the prospect of being able to get better, I'd come up against a brick wall and it was all hopeless after all. When I left the clinic I felt completely alone. The only help I thought might be available to me just wasn't there, and there seemed to be no one else to turn to. The depression came back with a vengeance and the next few months passed in a blur.

It was partly because I felt so alone after having pinned all my hopes on my appointment at the Priory Clinic that I eventually allowed the media to persuade me to do more interviews. I thought it might be a way of getting some help for myself, but afterwards it never seemed as though it had been worth it – until the letters started arriving. Although I always felt awful when a programme was aired or an article appeared in a newspaper or magazine, the really lovely letters I received from people made it all seem worthwhile again. People would write to me saying things like, 'I felt like I wanted to commit suicide. I was going to hang myself yesterday, until I saw you in the paper. I've cut out the article and stuck it on my bedroom wall as an inspiration to me and to remind me that I'm not alone.' They were wonderful letters, and people would also send me photographs and I'd think, 'You know what, I do know what I look like, and I do know how I feel about the article, but actually it's been worth the pain. I go through the pain every day anyway, so I might as well use it to help people.'

One of the shows I was asked to appear on was GMTV's *LK Today* with Lorraine Kelly. It started off really badly for me, because they made me sit with my back to the camera so that they could do a shot of the back of my head while they said, 'This girl is going to be on the show. She thinks X, Y and Z about herself,' and then they were going to do a reveal. It wasn't a good style for me, because I was sure that when I turned round and everyone saw my face they'd think, 'Hmm, I can see why she feels that way.' But in fact they talked about the issue really seriously and it went very well.

Then, as soon as that was over, I was asked to do a recording for ITV's *London Tonight* on the same day. I didn't really want to do it, because they were going to record outside, in the daylight. But Mum was insistent and, because the show with Lorraine Kelly had gone well, I was feeling a bit more relaxed and calm about it all, so I eventually agreed. But when I got home and watched the GMTV show on video, I went mad. First it was this picture of the back of my head and then I turned round looking disgusting. Although I still always had my hair over my face like a curtain, I'd become a bit more vocal by this point and was trying to speak up for myself. So, when they asked me how I felt, I said, 'I just feel I look different from everybody else.'

As I watched the video I was thinking, 'And I do!' I thought everyone would say, 'She *does* look like a freak. No wonder she feels like that.' I was really upset and said to Mum, 'If *London Tonight* show the film, I'll kill myself. If you let them air it, you'll have killed your daughter.'

So of course she phoned them and I think they understood what a serious issue it was, because they were really good and agreed not to air the film they'd taken of me.

Every time I watched a programme afterwards, I'd regret everything and have a really bad BDD attack. But then the letters would start coming in and they'd make me feel it had been worth it after all.

Shortly after doing the show with Lorraine Kelly, when I was still feeling very low, I was contacted by someone from an ITV chat show called *Vanessa*, which was hosted by Vanessa Feltz, but I couldn't be persuaded to do it for love nor money. In fact, I was lucky with most of the shows, because there was usually enough time between them to allow me to get over the ordeal and start to feel better again. But this time there hadn't been, and there really was no chance I was ever going to agree to do it.

As usual, though, Mum tried to persuade me, and said there was a car coming to collect me the following day. But this time I just said, 'No,' and refused to go. Although I felt bad about letting everyone down, I could sometimes be very hard about it and if I really didn't want to go, nothing would persuade me.

It also depended to some extent on how I was treated: if they were lovely people, which a lot of the producers were, they'd make me feel a bit more comfortable about it, and also I'd be even more reluctant to let them down. But if they seemed to be a bit calculating and it was obvious they weren't really interested in me and my feelings about things, but just in getting me on the show for their own purposes, I wouldn't do it. However, it also depended on what sort of day I was having: there were days when I could just about be persuaded to leave the house, and other days when absolutely nothing would lure me out.

Mum was like a lunatic, though: she'd go mad if I refused to do something. I think she felt as though I was getting some sort of therapy and that it kept me alive and safe. Every time I did a programme, it seemed to her that she wasn't having to deal with me all on her own; there were other people who knew about me and about what I was going through – as well as about what she was going through as a mother. Every time I locked myself away in my room in the dark, she must have been afraid that I wouldn't be alive in the morning. So maybe she was somehow sharing that anxiety with other people when they were also made aware of my existence and my problems.

Then one day I was contacted by someone from The *Trisha* show, who asked if my mum and a friend would go on her ITV show with me to talk about how my illness affected them. Trisha Goddard had recently come over from Australia and it was going to be her first show in this country. Because she met me for the first time when I was very ill – when I wouldn't speak and just sat there with my hair over my face – and because I was on her first show, she always remembers me and is really proud of me now. She knows just how ill I was and I think she realises that people look at me now and think, 'Oh, she couldn't have been all that ill,' because I was on her programme again recently and she mentioned that first show and said, 'I remember how Racheal had to be dragged on kicking and screaming.'

Trisha's a really caring and nice person. On that first show she could see I was in a state and didn't want to do it, so she came to speak to me in the Green Room before it started and made me feel more relaxed. Talking to her was like talking to a really sympathetic counsellor. Then, after the show, she took the time to sit and talk to me again and actually try to help me. On some of these programmes, like *The Time, The Place* for example, the hosts talk in a matter-of-fact way and then just say, 'OK, thanks, goodbye.' They don't show any feelings and don't seem to have any emotional connection with their guests. But Trisha's such a calming person and she made me feel safe, which is why I'll always go back to her now.

That first time I felt that, if she'd been through so much and could still do a show, I could do it too. But it wasn't easy. We had to go to a hotel the night before, but I think I must have been having a bad day, because after agreeing to do it I suddenly decided that I didn't want to. Mum said, 'Just come to the hotel and see how you feel in the morning,' and I kept telling myself that it wouldn't be so bad, because I'd have Mum and Belinda with me.

One funny thing that happened when we were having dinner at the hotel was that someone came over to our table and asked me if I'd be a dancer in their Prince tribute band. I thanked them politely, but said I wasn't interested at all, and Mum said, 'You see!

If you were really awful, people wouldn't want you to do something like that.'

The next morning I still really didn't want to do the show, which was hard for Mum and Belinda because they'd got themselves ready. I remember that I felt fat. I was trying on lots of different tops and nothing looked right, and I thought people would say, 'Yeah, I can completely understand why she doesn't want to leave the house!' That's how I'd feel on a bad day, which was why it was important that I felt strong rather than just OK. If I wasn't feeling strong, it was all just too much to deal with.

However, I forced myself to do the show, and I was really pleased I had, because Trisha was just so nice to me. She knew I was nervous, and when she came into the Green Room and saw that I was in tears she said, 'Racheal, you've been so brave.' She sat and talked to me and gave me the incentive to say, 'I'm going to do this,' because I knew I couldn't let her down and ruin her first show.

So I went through with it, but I wasn't in the mood to talk, although in fact that didn't matter too much because Belinda and Mum did most of the talking anyway. The moment I hated most was when Trisha said, 'Is there anyone in the audience who thinks this girl's ugly?' I was mortified, and thought, 'Oh my God. Someone's going to stand up in a minute and say something.' But fortunately no one did, although that just made me think they were all lying. I hated any sort of compliment because I'd think, 'I know what I am and I know I need to learn to deal with it.' What I saw in the mirror was skin on my face that looked as though it had been really badly burned, and by complimenting me people were in effect saying, 'No. It's not there.' I'd think, 'I know it is. So please don't make me feel as though I'm insane.'

I received loads of letters after *The Trisha Show*, which was really great. I think it was good to have Mum and a close friend there too, as it showed what it was like from the perspective of people who have to cope with someone with the illness, which meant that other people could identify with them. It's really difficult for anyone involved with a BDD sufferer, because they can so easily say the wrong thing. They must feel worried every time they open their mouths that something they might say could lead to the person killing themselves – and that's a dreadful responsibility.

I went on *The Trisha Show* again recently, to talk to a girl called Louisa who's really quite ill and has been suicidal. I think it was a straight choice for her: either to do the show and try to get help or to kill herself. I'd just arrived back from Spain that morning and was exhausted – my skin was terrible and I felt awful – but I thought, 'If this girl wants me, I'll go.' Feeling I can do some good – after spending so much of my life thinking I was an awful person – is really the only thing that gets me out of bed in the morning. People thank me for helping them, but the truth is that I have more to thank them for, because without them I wouldn't have got better myself. When Louisa asked me, 'Why do you want to help me? Why do you think I'm worth helping?' I told her, 'Because I see potential in you, and I see you *can* get better. But actually, don't think I'm just helping you, because by helping you I'm also helping myself.' It may sound a strange thing to say, but helping someone else get better makes me feel that I'm a real person.

I've stayed in touch with Louisa, and talking to her also helps me to see things from another perspective, because I'm not a trained counsellor or psychologist, and I never know whether I'm saying the right thing. I told her that our illnesses were obviously similar, but that they might well differ in some respects and all I can do is talk to her about my experience of BDD and how I dealt with it. I'm giving her daily goals, which is going really well, and I've tried to explain to her that, no matter how much surgery BDD sufferers have, they'll feel exactly the same, because it's all in their heads.

The good thing is that Louisa's probably stronger than I was,

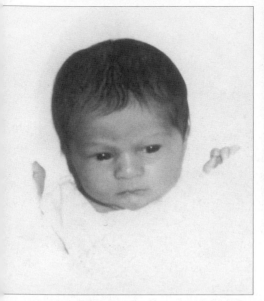

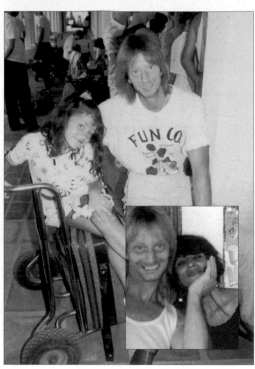

Above left: Only four hours old.

Above right: On the croquet lawn at my childhood home in Burstow, Surrey.

Below left: My brother, Jason, tried to increase my confidence by using me as a model for his photography practice.

Below right: Even though he was a workaholic, my dad, Tony, found time for family holidays.

Inset: Dad and my mum, Jenny – Mum's tenacity and determination were to help me through troubled times in later years.

Above: As a child, my passion was for animals. Here I am with my brother, James, and two friends.

Below: School was not a particularly happy place for me but James looked out for me as much as he could.

My love of animals meant that our house was something of a menagerie …

Above left: One of our dogs, Major.

Above right: My beautiful kitten was run over by my mum – she hadn't realised that he was asleep on the wheel of the car.

Below: Tigger, another of our many dogs!

The beautiful house at Burstow, where I grew up.

Above: The horsey girl – the only time I felt comfortable was when I was wearing my riding gear.

Below left: My best friend, Fay Greene, who taught me the greatest lesson I will ever learn – that life is a gift that should not be taken for granted.

Below right: With such a large and sociable family, our house was always filled with people, such as at this fancy dress party held by my parents one Christmas.

Pictures of myself which I defaced because I hated what I saw in them, particularly my nose.

Above left: As a bridesmaid at my brother Geoff's wedding. I am on the far right, not looking very comfortable.

Above right: Paul aged 20, when I first met him.

Below: Paul and me in Scotland with his grandmother.

Above: My four big brothers were a huge support to me during those dark years. *Clockwise from top left*: James, Jason, Andrew and Geoff.

Below: Me aged 17 and 18 – I look painfully thin, but I'd actually started to gain a bit of weight by this time.

because when I was ill I didn't want to talk to people about it at all. I'd talk to the Samaritans, because they didn't know who I was, but otherwise I'd let my mum do all the talking, and, if another girl had given me her details and suggested I contact her, I wouldn't have done so. But, although Louisa hides her face under her hair, she's a real chatterbox, and I think with the right help she could do really well.

When we were recording the show, I started to cry as I was listening to Louisa talking, and the counsellor who was there gave me a hug. She was a really lovely woman, and beautiful, so I was very surprised when she said that when she was young she always used to think she was unattractive, and that she hated herself and had eating disorders and all sorts of problems. Apparently, she was looking at a photograph recently when her husband walked past and said, 'Oh, isn't that a beautiful picture of you,' and she said, 'No. It's not me; it's Chrissie [her daughter].' Then she looked at it again and saw that it did look just like her when she was younger, and when she put it together with an actual photograph of her young self the two looked identical. She knew her daughter was beautiful, so she felt very sad that she'd wasted her life not realising that what she used to see when she looked at herself wasn't real, and it was ironic that she only became aware of that when she saw herself in her daughter.

During the period when I was doing the TV shows and newspaper articles, I was still very ill. But they enabled me to take the first tentative steps towards understanding that, like many other people, I had an illness that was distorting my perception of myself. Although I sank into depression after each one, I'd then receive the letters and would start to feel that perhaps I could do something worthwhile with my life after all.

12

A New Relationship

I did occasionally manage to go out with friends, but only at night, and only to dark nightclubs wearing one of my long black coats. At 16 I shouldn't really have been going to these places at all, but I think my parents didn't try to stop me because they were so anxious for me to do *something* that normal teenagers did. Of course, at that age I shouldn't have been drinking alcohol either, but one of my reasons for going to nightclubs was that it gave me access to alcohol, which helped switch off the pain that was otherwise always with me.

Although drinking sometimes made me feel better, at other times it would have the opposite effect and I'd get in such a state about what I looked like that I'd smash a glass and cut my arms to pieces. Then I'd end up halfway through the evening crying in the toilets and have to go home.

I'd try so hard to go out, but often I'd do what I used to call 'deteriorating'. I'd think I looked OK for a while, that I'd got my make-up the way I wanted it, but after about an hour it all started deteriorating and I'd have to keep going to the toilets every five minutes to try to put it right. Other girls would then notice me and think I was vain and say, 'Oh, look at her, always putting make-up on. She loves herself.' Understandably, they assumed I was doing it because I thought I looked great, when in fact it was the complete opposite. So inevitably people didn't accept me, and they'd whisper about me behind my back, although I don't know how much of that was simply my perception clouded by alcohol. But I do remember one occasion when I was a little bit stronger and I said to one girl, 'Do you know what? You probably love yourself more than I do, because you're out without make-up and I can't come out at all without this on.'

Unfortunately, she took it the wrong way and grabbed hold of me and hissed, 'You're ugly. Don't you ever forget that. You look like a cat.'

I usually went to the nightclubs with my friend who suffered from a sort of agoraphobia-like social anxiety. She was the only person who could really persuade me to leave the house, because she was the only person outside my family I trusted, and I knew that going out was hard for her too. We only went once a month at most, and when we did it was always a big deal and I really wanted to look my best.

One day, not long before I was 17, my friend begged me to go to a nightclub with her but I told her I couldn't because I didn't have any shoes to wear. When I was having one of my rages I'd throw things and break them, and during a recent panic attack I'd broken the heels of my shoes. But she kept begging me to go with her and, because I knew that if she didn't go out she became more and more depressed, I finally decided I'd make a quick visit to Crawley to buy some shoes for the evening.

Walking towards the town centre I passed a couple of builders who shouted, 'Oi, ugly. If you were better looking we might want your number. But you just ain't got the looks, sweetheart.'

I was devastated. I was feeling bad enough anyway, and I

desperately wanted to turn round and go home. But instead, to get out of public view as quickly as possible, I rushed into the first shop I saw in Crawley Mall, which happened to be a shoe shop and which, mercifully, was empty.

I thought I'd quickly buy some shoes and then get out of there and go home, so I asked the assistant if he had any sandals. He showed me some really disgusting ones and said, 'Only these. They're the only ones we're going to have all season.' I was desperate to get home, so, although they were awful, I bought them and fled.

It was really hard for me to go out that night, not least because I couldn't get the remarks the builders had made to me out of my mind. I was really depressed and had a migraine, but I knew my friend would be upset if I didn't go, so I put on a long black jacket and black trousers, big red fake nails and loads and loads of make-up. When we arrived at the nightclub I didn't socialise at all; I just kept my head down on the table, hiding my face.

After a while my friend said, 'That boy from the shoe shop is looking at you.'

'No he's not,' I groaned. 'I just want to go home.' But a few minutes later he walked past us and looked me straight in the face, although I was still convinced he was looking at my friend.

She's always loved singing and dancing, and when she got up and started dancing around on her own I was left standing alone at the side of the dance floor. Suddenly a man sauntered over and asked if I had a cigarette, and the next thing I knew the guy from the shoe shop, who obviously thought the man was hassling me, was at my side saying firmly, 'She's with me, mate.'

I was really shocked that he'd come over to talk to me, and the only thing I could think of saying to him was, 'I've got a bone to pick with you. The heel on one of the shoes I bought from you is almost broken. Are you sure you didn't have any others coming in?' And he just laughed.

Then, after a few minutes, I said to him, 'It was lovely to meet you, but I'm going to go home.' I signalled to my friend, and as we started to leave he said, 'I can give you a lift if you want one.' Going off with a total stranger is probably not the best thing to do in any circumstances, but I felt I could trust him, so I accepted his offer. Although I thought he was a really nice and polite boy, when we reached my house I jumped out of the car with a hasty 'Goodbye. Thank you very much,' and disappeared inside, not even knowing his name.

The next day I was round at my friend's house, wearing my blobs, when my mum phoned and said, 'A boy's turned up, Racheal. He's come from Brighton, and his name's Paul. Do you want to come back home?'

'I don't know who he is,' I told her. 'No, I'm not coming back.'

It didn't matter who he was: I wasn't prepared to see anyone without my make-up on and, as it would take me five hours to do it, there was no way I was going to go home.

Apparently, he sat chatting to my parents for about three hours, but he'd left when I finally did get home, and it was only from my parents' description that I realised it was the boy from the shoe shop. My dad said, 'Oh, by the way, he left his number,' which was really strange because my dad had never accepted any boys before. But he seemed to like Paul. I hadn't asked him to come and I didn't want to phone him, but Dad insisted, saying, 'It's really rude not to after he came all this way to see you.'

So I eventually phoned Paul to apologise about not going back home while he was there, and I think I made some excuse about not being well. But by the end of the phone call we'd agreed to meet the next day, and when he arrived I'd covered my face in layers and layers of make-up and was wearing fake nails, which he admired. I didn't tell him they weren't my real nails, which turned out to be rather a mistake, because for the next year or so I had to put them on quickly if he ever turned up unannounced.

A New Relationship

The funny thing about Paul is that he's quite happy just to sleep, and our first date consisted pretty much of him dozing while we watched television in the dark. After that he came round every night, but it would always be dark when he saw me; we never had any dates in the daytime.

Then one day he said to me, 'I think you'd look really pretty without your lipstick on.'

To call it 'lipstick' was somewhat of an understatement, as in reality it was almost-black lip liner and loads of very dark-red lipstick. It felt as though he was criticising my whole image, but, although I felt a bit tearful and panicky, I didn't want to make a big deal of it, so I just said, 'Oh, I don't want to take it off.'

Over the next couple of weeks, he asked me again, and when I finally did take it off he said, 'You look much prettier like that. You don't need it.'

That was quite an important moment for me, because it felt as though it was the first time someone who wasn't a member of my family thought I looked OK with part of my naturalness showing. Partly as a result of the bullying I'd experienced, it seemed that my whole life I'd felt the need to wear a disguise so that people didn't see the real me and judge me. So it was really nice to feel that someone thought I looked all right without at least a part of it.

It was a long time before I let Paul stay the night, because I didn't want him to see me without my make-up. Then, when I did finally agree, it was an absolute nightmare, because I'd wear the make-up to bed and have to get up the next morning and put more on over the top of it – which took hours and meant I didn't get much sleep. But over a period of about two months he persuaded me to take off more and more of it, although I never reached the point of being completely without it. (For me, 'no make-up' simply meant wearing fewer layers, and I still wore eyeliner, mascara and blusher.)

To put all this into some sort of perspective, not even my family could see me without my make-up on, so it was a huge step to let myself be seen like that by someone outside the family, particularly as it then meant I had to let the family see me like that too. But I still wore the blobs over the make-up, and the number of blobs I was wearing was an indication of how I was feeling on a particular day. If they were all over my whole face, I was having a bad day; if there weren't very many, I was having an OK day.

When I said to Paul, 'You met me when I was wearing all this make-up, so why do you want me to take it off?' his reply was, 'Because I could see you didn't need it, and that underneath it you were beautiful.'

But in fact it was four years before he saw me without any make-up, because my skin was still a massive issue to me. No matter how clear people said it was, I was convinced I had really severe acne, like a disease on my face that had to be covered up and camouflaged at all times.

Paul knew I'd never agree to go anywhere, but I don't think he really understood what was going on. Then one day he wanted to go out to rent a video and when I told him, 'I'm not coming unless I can come with blobs of talc on my face,' he said, 'No, Racheal. It's only going to draw attention to you even more!'

So I tied a tie round my head, Rambo style, and said, 'Well, can I come with that on?' I don't know what I was trying to achieve. But Paul said, 'No,' and I shouted, 'Well, I'm not coming then,' and started getting a panic attack.

I look back on it now and can laugh, but at the time I was completely serious. Poor boy! He must have been thinking, 'What the hell is wrong with this girl?' I had a fit and went absolutely mad and threw an ironing board at him. I was screaming, crying and kicking and then locked myself in the bedroom, and I think that was when Mum had to explain to him what was wrong with me, although even then I don't think he understood – and I don't think he really understands now. But at least knowing I was ill helped him to deal with it all a bit better.

When Paul discovered that I sometimes cut myself, he said, 'If you do it again, I'm going to leave you.' I tried to explain to him that I never meant to do it, that it wasn't as though I'd sit there and decide, 'I'm going to cut myself,' but sometimes I'd just black out and it wasn't something I could control. But he didn't really understand.

13

Creating Awareness

Some time after we'd cancelled the airing of the *London Tonight* recording, someone from the ITV programme *This Morning* got in touch. Mum eventually managed to persuade me to do the show by saying, 'You've half helped people and you've half helped yourself, but now you have to finish what you've started.' She was right in a way, because by this point there were a lot of people looking to me as a spokesperson, as someone who might be able to get them some help by stimulating some under-standing about BDD. My ambition was for people to be able to walk into a doctor's surgery and say, 'I think I'm suffering from BDD,' and for the doctor not to look at them blankly and ask, 'What's BDD?' That's how it was when I was ill, and when I go to see my doctor now he shakes my hand and says he's very proud of me.

I'd also had enough time to recover after doing the last programme by then, and I felt I could try to be strong again. But the real reason I did the show was because there was going to be a boy on it who'd gone through the same sorts of things as me.

Apparently, he'd seen me on the programmes I'd already done, and that's what made him agree to talk.

I'd never heard of a boy suffering from BDD before – although I now know that there are many boys and men with the illness – so I was really interested to meet him, and also just to meet another sufferer face to face for the first time. I'd seen pictures of other BDD sufferers and read their letters, but I'd never actually spoken to one of them in person.

I'll always remember turning up at the show and seeing Stephen. He was there with his girlfriend, who was lovely, and he was really good-looking. He had beautiful bone structure, a perfect face, but he'd tried to give himself a facelift with a staple gun. I was completely shocked and really felt for him. Also, it made me think that, if he couldn't see what a striking-looking boy he was, perhaps I was seeing something in myself that was different from what other people saw. Maybe what I was seeing when I looked in the mirror wasn't real.

Stephen kept his head down all the time and didn't want to look at anyone or make eye contact, and I realised we were two of a kind. I was very shy and nervous on the programme myself, but I was able to talk a bit, which shows how far I'd come. Seeing someone of the opposite sex with the same sorts of problems and mannerisms as I had was quite scary, because I suppose I'd assumed that it was only women who suffered from insecurity about their appearance. But it made me realise that men can feel the same way and are perhaps even less able than women to talk about it openly.

Being on the show together was really quite bizarre because, when someone tried to compliment us, we both did the same thing at the same time. When I watched the video afterwards, I didn't feel as bad as I usually did, because, although I hated what I looked like, I was focused on Stephen. But, as usual, I didn't simply watch it; I kept pausing it until Mum eventually said,

'People aren't going to analyse it like you, Racheal. You don't have to keep doing that.'

I don't know why I made myself sit through it; I suppose it was just another obsession. But I also found the things Stephen was saying really comforting, and hoped that if he watched it too, he'd focus on me rather than on himself and would feel the same way. It also made me wonder if I was giving other people the same sort of inspiration I was getting from Stephen. It's so nice to feel that you're not alone, and even nicer when you actually meet someone similar to you.

Meeting Stephen also made me consider the possibility that my illness really could be due to a chemical imbalance in my brain that was making me see something that wasn't there, because there was absolutely nothing wrong with the way he looked. He had really chiselled features and could easily have been a catwalk model. So it was just shocking to see what he was doing to himself and how much pain he was suffering, and no doubt his family too.

After the programme I was inundated with letters, which again made me feel it had all been worthwhile. By this stage there was a bit more known about BDD, and awareness of it had begun to spread.

At around this time I also took part in a documentary called *Best Friends*, which was about people who'd been through difficult times and the friends who'd stood by them. They wanted to film me going about my everyday life and to talk to one of my friends about her experiences of having to deal with someone with BDD.

Although I understand now why Mum did it, I felt she'd been forcing me to do all this media stuff when I really didn't want to, and I didn't want to do this documentary either. But by this stage I'd realised that the more I got out there and showed people what my life was like, the more people I could help. So this seemed like an opportunity to let people see what I actually had to go through, and then perhaps they'd understand how difficult it could be for other people like me.

It was around the end of 1999; I'd moved with my family from Burstow, Paul had helped me reach the stage of being more comfortable about being seen, and I was getting more used to trying to be brave.

Although the programme didn't really seem to be a good thing to do from my own personal point of view, I told the producer I'd do it as long as they didn't film me in Crawley, because I didn't want local people to see me. So they took me to East Grinstead, which in itself shows how far I'd come in my recovery, because previously I'd never have gone there.

When we arrived in East Grinstead, I walked into a bar and some guy immediately started giving me abuse, calling me ugly and shouting at me. The camera crew had been filming from a distance, and when they suddenly appeared I burst into tears. They tried to carry on filming me while I was crying, but I couldn't bear it and told them, 'I've got to go home. You made me come here. I don't want to talk. I don't want to carry on with this documentary.'

Although I was really upset, it was good in one way because it actually showed people what I went through every day, and that I wasn't imagining it. I just don't understand why people did that sort of thing to me, and can only think it's because I look a bit miserable; I'm not naturally very smiley. Or perhaps I look stuck-up and in need of bringing down a peg or two, but that's only because I'm shy. I don't know why I had to go through all those abusive attacks by people, but when the documentary was shown on TV they just looked like a bunch of idiots, and at least it must have made it clear to people why I rarely went out.

It was a small film crew and they were really lovely. They filmed me doing all my rituals and putting on the white blobs, which I thought drew attention away from my face. When you're doing a documentary, it doesn't feel as though you're on TV, and, although it was hard in a lot of respects, it was also quite therapeutic, because I was opening up and showing people snapshots of my life. I'm pretty sure I couldn't have done it during the worst of my illness, but I'd reached the point of being maybe a quarter of the way through the journey towards recovery. I'd spoken about BDD so much that I'd started to become detached from it and to see it as an illness rather than as part of me.

I think it also helped that the focus of the programme wasn't me having to talk about BDD, but rather actually showed what I did each day. There were still days when I wouldn't come out of my room and they showed those too, as well as people trying to coax me out and what Paul and Belinda had to say about it all.

In fact, it was on that programme that Belinda complained about me not sending her a birthday card, and apparently there were some other things she said that they decided to cut out. But one of the more sympathetic comments she made on camera was: 'It's difficult to watch everybody else having a life and Racheal just fading into oblivion.'

14

A Surgical Solution?

I'd always begged Mum and Dad to let me have surgery, to get myself 'fixed', but, quite rightly, they refused. Then, about a year after the article appeared in the *Daily Mail* and I'd had my disappointing consultation at the Priory Clinic, a company called September Films contacted me and said they'd like to take me to Cambridge to have a surgical consultation for a nose job. It was what I so desperately wanted, because I thought it was the one thing that would allow me to sort myself out. Obviously, surgery is the worst thing in the world to offer a BDD sufferer, but no one knew that then because there simply wasn't enough known about the illness at the time.

They were planning to make a programme along the lines of *Extreme Makeover*, and to film the consultation, surgery and recovery period, and I agreed to do it purely for what it would give me. Still only 16, I was too young to give legal consent, but I told the producers I was 19. Although I hated the idea of being filmed, I was so desperate to look different that I felt it would be a price worth paying. I certainly couldn't have afforded to pay for that sort of surgery myself, and as my parents were very much against me having it done, they weren't going to pay for it either, although they did eventually agree to my taking part in the film. I think they'd reached the point of mental exhaustion and were thinking, 'Just go with whatever she wants.' They probably felt that at least surgery might make me happy, and I know that's a feeling shared by other parents of BDD sufferers: they become so desperate that they're prepared to try anything to make their children's lives more bearable.

But, as I say, it's the worst thing a BDD sufferer can do. I know now that, no matter what I change about myself, there'll always be something new to focus on. I realise I'm never going to be happy with my face, so all I can do is learn to live with it the way it is. Even now, I sometimes look in the mirror and think about getting some part of my face 'fixed', but I know that if I do, there'll always be some other feature that needs fixing. For example, however much people tell me otherwise, I still think I've got massive bags under my eyes, but now when I start to worry about them I'm able to tell myself, 'Stop it! You know it's just you.' However, I didn't realise any of that at the time, and I was convinced surgery was the answer.

The production team were really lovely people, probably the nicest film crew I've ever met, and I was really excited as I travelled to Cambridge with them in a van to see the surgeon. Previously I wouldn't have left the house for a million pounds, but I'd taken the first small steps towards recovery by this time and, because it was something I'd always longed to do, it wasn't all that hard – and it turned out to be a very interesting experience.

When I saw the doctor, he showed me 'before' and 'after' pictures on a computer to give me an idea of what I'd look like when I'd had my nose fixed and, to my amazement, I didn't like the 'after'. It was a real eye-opener because, having wanted surgery for literally years, I would never have believed I wouldn't go through with it. The decision I made was probably partly due to the fact that I was afraid of the operation being shown on television. I didn't want people saying, 'Oh, she's only pretty because she's had her nose done.' But there was more to it than that.

Something I'd never even considered was that the nose in the 'after' picture didn't suit me, and I immediately began thinking, 'If I had that nose, I'd need a bigger chin, so I'd have to have a chin implant. Then I'd have to have my eyes made less big and round...' But what was the point of starting something that was probably never going to stop? I suddenly realised that surgery wasn't going to make me feel better. I have the letters people wrote to me to thank for that decision. For the past year, I'd been writing to people who felt they were disfigured, and the pictures they sent me had gradually made me start to accept that what I was seeing in myself was an illusion.

So, as it turned out, visiting the surgeon was the beginning of a remarkable turning point for me. Having been forced to accept that surgery wouldn't fix my problem, I began to analyse things and realise I had to help myself.

I didn't know then that there are people who undergo serial cosmetic surgery and are never able to stop. I just knew as I sat looking at the computer in the doctor's consultation room that it would be only the first of many operations, each one serving to highlight other disfigurements that had previously been less obvious.

The hard thing about being me is that I've always wanted to be something completely different, the opposite of what I actually am – and that's almost never achievable for anyone. It's not as simple as wanting to be a blonde or a redhead; it's a passionate desire to be someone else entirely. I know now that I'm never going to be what I want to be, and that I have to learn to accept what I am and get on with my life.

I was a bit nervous about the prospect of telling the film crew that I didn't want to go ahead with the operation, but they were very supportive. It was almost as though they'd gone through it all to make me see that it wasn't the solution for me, and if that was the case – which is very unlikely – it worked on a massive scale.

However, the realisation that surgery wasn't the answer didn't have an immediately positive impact on me, as I was very stressed about it all. Having driven to Cambridge with the film crew, with whom I felt safe, I had to go home alone on the train, because, of course, they were continuing to film the documentary. I was very ill during the journey and felt very panicky about being on my own. Although by this time there were certain places I could go and feel secure, I didn't feel safe alone on the train and I started having really bad stomach cramps and spent most of the journey in the toilet, crying my eyes out.

Part of the reason I was so upset was because I kept thinking, 'Oh my God, what am I going to do?' I'd really thought that surgery was going to be the solution and that it would make everything better. So I was very disappointed when I realised it wouldn't make a blind bit of difference. In fact, I felt almost as though I'd had it done and it hadn't worked. But the experience did force me to accept that the only way I was going to fix things was to change how I felt, not what I looked like.

After that, I went downhill and became very depressed and reluctant to do anything for about six months. I was also really scared, because I thought that when the programme came out everyone would know I wanted surgery. I'd gone to Cambridge thinking that wouldn't matter, because the operation would have been done and the illness would be over. But, in a way, not having had it done was the worst of all worlds, because when the documentary was screened everyone would know I didn't like my nose, and that would make them focus on it all the more. In fact, what's ironic is that, after the programme was shown, lots of people thought I'd had the surgery anyway, and even now I hear people say, 'Oh, look, that's the girl who had the nose job on TV.'

15

A Reality Check

Shortly after *Best Friends* was shown on television, I did *The Maury Show* in America. I think they'd done some research on the Internet and some stories had come up about me, so they looked up my phone number. But the only person who came up under Baughan was my brother James, so they contacted him initially and he put them in touch with me.

I was really scared at the prospect of doing the show with Maury Povich, particularly because it was on a much larger scale than anything I'd done before. But I thought it would be worthwhile because it might be a chance for me to get some real help. Much more was known about BDD in America than here, and I knew there were going to be other people like me on the show.

When the producers contacted me, I told them I couldn't go without my mum, so she came with me and they put us up in a hotel in New York the night before. I was very nervous, although quite excited during the taxi ride, but when I went on the show I completely lost it. I couldn't speak and just cried the whole time. I'd reached the point of usually being able to be relatively strong and give some sort of answer to almost any question, but I really went backwards that day. What I think tipped the balance was listening to other people like me talking; I couldn't bear to watch them going through what I'd been through. There was one particular young girl of about 14 who was really ill and I felt a terrible responsibility to say something inspiring, and then couldn't. I think there was a counsellor on the show and she tried to talk to me, but the whole experience is just a blur; I can't really remember how I was feeling or what happened. Then, after all that, having not even opened my mouth on the show, I tripped on the stairs as I was leaving and ended up feeling even more stupid.

After that trip to New York, I was mentally drained and really disappointed with myself. Thankfully I never saw the show aired, because that would probably have made me feel even worse. I think that to some extent I was trying to fake my recovery, to make out I was better than I actually was, and you can't do that. I felt I should be helping other people, but I simply wasn't ready to do it, because I still needed help myself. I was trying to run before I could walk, and it was just too soon to attempt to do something that big. It was really frustrating because I knew in my head all the things I wanted to say, and I really wanted to use it as an opportunity to get the sort of help that was available in America, but you have to accept that it isn't going to work out well all the time.

So doing *The Maury Show* was a real ordeal for me. Although I'd begun to be more able to talk about things, and had been interviewed for a lot of magazine articles by then, for some reason I just couldn't handle it. Perhaps it was something to do with jetlag and being tired, and also with the pressure of being flown out to America. I didn't have the security I always had in England of being able to say 'No' if I changed my mind at the last minute, and I felt even more strongly than usual that I couldn't let them down.

After that, *The Montel Williams Show* got in touch, but I did turn that one down. My brother thought I should do it, but I said, 'I didn't gain anything from doing *Maury*. I just felt awful. So I don't want to put myself through that again.'

Fortunately, I realised I had to think of myself to some degree, and not do things that were guaranteed to make me feel worse. I know my brother and my mum thought I might be able to get help if I did more in America, because there were psychologists there who knew so much more about BDD than anyone here. But, after my experience with the BDD specialist at the Priory Clinic, I'd convinced myself that no one could help me, and it was always at the back of my mind that any other doctor would be just like him. So I wasn't as optimistic as they were about what talking to psychologists might do for me.

Although I did do TV programmes and interviews for magazine and newspaper articles in the hope that they'd help other people, and, in the early days, that they might also be a means of finding help for me, I did feel very much alone after my visit to the specialist. I'd been comforted to some extent by the fact that there was a name for what I suffered from, but I doubted whether any psychologist or counsellor would be able to help me, and I didn't want to take anti-depressants because of what I'd seen them do to my mum. So I gradually began to realise that *I* was the only one who could help myself.

Although I still wished I could be dead and Fay could be alive, I knew by this point that I had to try to do my best to make the most of my life. I desperately wanted to get better because I didn't want to live the way I was, so obsessed about what I looked like when I'd always thought looks were the last thing on my mind, and so afraid that people were going to judge me.

In fact, something I'd completely forgotten about until I

recently came across a little silver notebook I'd called 'Racheal's depression book, 1999–2000' is that, for a short period during the early days of my recovery, I used to write down my emotions. I'd decided that, whenever I felt a BDD attack coming on, I'd scribble down how I was feeling as a way of trying to release the pain inside me. By this time I'd made the decision that I wanted to stop self-harming and get better, so I used the writing as a kind of therapy, and would also draw pictures of how I saw myself. I suppose it was a way of helping to release all the horrible thoughts that were swirling around my mind. I'd be in a rage when I started to write, but reading it back would gradually start to calm me down. It gave me a feeling of comfort because it helped me to detach myself from the BDD and see it as something in my head rather than it being me. I'd feel it was the BDD that 'told' me to write those things and that BDD was making me feel the way I felt, so I thought that if I could detach myself from it, it might go away. I felt very sad each time I read what I'd written, because it seemed as though I was reading about someone else's feelings, someone I really wanted to help.

Some pages from the silver notebook

Throughout this book I will proceed to set myself daily goals. I will then compare my feelings from day to day to see if I am making progress and I will explain how it feels to have body dysmorphic disorder in reality with detail.

Each insult will be listed and each compliment, then I will compare them together to see which of the two I receive most. I intend to write in this book for the next 2 years in the hope that by the time I have finished I will have made great progress and will be able to help other people with this disorder get better too.

Maybe I won't ever get better, but if nothing else, writing in this book will be my only way of expressing my feelings without having to upset the people that I love in the process.

I find that writing helps to prevent me cutting my arms, and when I am in a frantic state it calms me down to write everything I am feeling on to paper then read it over and over until I am calm again. It is also a lot safer than cutting my arms and will not leave the nasty scars.

Well this will be the beginning of my recovery and I am hoping that by the end of this book it will also be the end of the constant pain I feel in my mind.

The people at present in my life are my mother Jenny, my father Tony, my brother James 23, my brother Jason 29, my brother Geoffrey 28, my brother Andrew 32, his girlfriend Nicky 21, my friends Belinda, Cathy, Hannah and Ann Marie, my boyfriend Paul, 21, and his mum Irine, his dad Bob and his sister Tracey, all of which I may speak about within this.

A page from the silver notebook written during an attack

I feel as though I am alone. No one cares or understands me. Why can't they see what I can see, or maybe they can! People are liars, they lie to make me feel better but it does not! I hate my life. Each day I wish to die. I do not want to be here. I am sometimes mistaken for being moody although it's not that I am moody, it's the hurt that I am feeling inside because of the fat grotesque bitch I see before me in the mirror. It's hard to smile when you have so much self hate! I have no trust in anyone now. I have been hurt too much. I wake up sometimes and I do not want to get out of bed as I feel that I am too much of a mutant to face the world with my ratty long hair, my evil, drugged-up looking eyes, massive nose, horrid lips, big stomach, fat legs. I don't deserve to be on this earth. Why was I punished with this face and body that ruin my life?

I didn't keep up the book for very long, and only completed a handful of pages, because in my state of panic during a BDD attack I wasn't always able to think clearly enough to be able to find it. But I did continue to write my emotions down on scraps of paper and anything else that came easily to hand. What I find interesting about looking at the book now is that it shows that by 1999 I had already become determined to help myself.

16

Trying to Pick Up the Pieces

Paul understood the regrets I had about my education having come to a premature end, and he'd say to me, 'There's no reason why you can't go back and try to make up for what you've missed out on.'

Mum was really keen on the idea too and eventually she went down to the local college to find out if they did make-up courses. Unfortunately, the nearest place was in London, and that was out of the question because I couldn't have gone anywhere that wasn't local enough for me to be able to get home quickly if I had a panic attack. But the local college did do a beauty course, so I decided to have a go at that, as it would at least give me some knowledge about the industry and some qualifications that might enable me to go on later and do a make-up artist's course.

I'd missed out on all my GCSEs and was starting to have very strong regrets about having allowed the bullying and my illness to pretty much halt my life in its tracks. So I decided I'd do maths and English as well as the beauty course. I was just plain bad at maths, but I was quite good at English, in terms of expressing myself, although my spelling and punctuation are very poor and so anything I wrote wasn't really readable, which was very frustrating. So, on one of my good days, I went along to the college in Crawley to register.

Paul's attitude was, 'If you can do all this stuff on TV because your mum makes you, I'm going to make you do this.' So they were both forcing me to do things they thought would help me, and I'd certainly never have done them if left to my own devices. It scares me when I think that there must be so many BDD sufferers who haven't had the sort of help I had, or whose families are afraid to force them to do things for fear of what effect it will have on them, and therefore they may end up never getting any better.

However, as with anything I thought I'd like to do, I still had to be dragged into doing it by Paul and my mum. Although the course was really good, going to college was a nightmare because there were still only certain people I would allow to see me without all my make-up on, and it took me five hours to get ready every day.

I suppose I'd always been fairly strange, but I became even stranger during my time at college. I'd wear bright and garish colours, for example green and purple together, and people used to make nasty comments and call me all sorts of names – and in fact that continued to some extent long after college, until I was about 23. I'd wear big fake eyelashes, long red nails, a red feather boa and a long black coat – like a very dedicated drag queen. In fact, I was covering up the person underneath, and I suppose that's what drag queens are doing in a way. I think some of them can be quite depressed when not in their role, and it was the same for me: when I was in my role I was comfortable, but if I didn't look right for the role I wanted to play, I couldn't go out, because I couldn't fake it. I felt trapped in my body and as though I was in the wrong body, and I just wanted to be free from it. Basically, it felt as though my personality and who I wanted to be didn't fit the body I'd been given.

Although I'd made massive progress by this time, there were still days when I couldn't go to college. One of the problems was having to face the same people who used to pick on me at school, which made it even more difficult to focus on my studies. So, every time I had an attack and couldn't go in, I'd miss important lessons, and I ended up missing so much maths and English that it became pointless to try to continue with them.

I did try really hard to carry on with the beauty course, because it was so important to me, but one day we were told that we would have to take our make-up off after lunch so that we could practise on one another. Obviously that couldn't happen, so I walked out at lunchtime and went home. The worry triggered an anxiety attack and I was in tears, thinking, 'Oh my God, what am I going to do now? How do I go back after lunch? How can I get out of having to take my make-up off?'

Mum phoned the college and tried to explain about my illness – and also about the fact that I had a very sensitive skin and wouldn't be able to use their products – and she asked if there was any way we could work round it. But it was like trying to tell someone about an illness they don't believe exists. They just didn't understand and said, 'No. Sorry. Everyone has to participate otherwise someone won't have a partner.'

It was really disappointing, because I was doing so well on the course and was a real natural at it – being a BDD sufferer, one thing I knew how to do was apply make-up, because I'd studied it my whole life and it was second nature.

Although the course was very good, and I learned a lot about the skin and various other things, it wasn't really what I'd wanted to do, as I was more interested in theatre make-up. So, when it came down to it, I suppose it wasn't really worth my attempting to overcome the enormous hurdle of even trying to do without my make-up. There'd been other silly little problems too, such as my insisting on wearing a long coat all the time and not being able to have a massage because I didn't want anyone to see my shoulders. So I suppose it wasn't really working out anyway. But that day was the final straw and I just couldn't continue – and that was the end of my college education.

I was devastated, because I realised that my face and my illness were holding me back from being able to do everything I ever wanted or tried to do. I know it sounds extreme, but it was like being disabled. I already felt as though I was disfigured and I wished my face could be burned off and that I didn't have one at all. I know people must have thought I was just being selfish, but it's difficult to understand how bad BDD sufferers feel about themselves. I was designing my own clothes at this stage, and I used to wish it would become fashionable to wear masked-ball costumes and to put little stick-on hearts and moons on your face. Then I could have used them to cover my spots – although I doubt whether it would ever have been the fashion to cover your face in them completely, which is what I would have needed to do.

After I stopped going to college, Mum found me an English tutor, who came to the house for about a month. He didn't know I had an illness, and it must have been very difficult for him when I kept cancelling every time I had a BDD attack. But, although my punctuation and spelling are still pretty bad, I learned a lot about writing from him in that month, including how to write poems.

When my attempt to go to college ended in such huge disappointment, it seemed to me that I failed at everything I tried to do. I'd made massive progress before I started there and, although I knew there'd be days when I couldn't go in, I never imagined I'd have to abandon the course completely, and that was really upsetting.

After my failed attempt to go to college, I did a story for the *Sunday People* newspaper. They rang Mum to see how I was

above left: While employed at Just GTIs, I felt able to reduce the amount of make up wore to cover my face.

above right: The photo that my mum sent to the Miss England competition, without e knowing!

elow: Support from the troops in Iraq.

Above: I was incredibly anxious about Miss England 2004 but managed to get myself through the sportswear and evening dress rounds.

Below: Miss Great Britain 2006 – the dreaded swimwear round. That's me at the back, third from the left.

ights! Camera! Action! My mantra helped me through many situations I found
hallenging – even today, though, I am much more comfortable in my own studio
here I can choose how the photos are taken.

Here, I am presenting Miss Limo 2006.

Below left: With my co-presenter and, *below right*, taking a well-earned rest. There was a time when I would simply have been unable to do many of the things I do now.

Above: With my mum, who is my mirror; I trust her to tell me if a photo isn't a good one.

Below: At True Model Media, I only employ models who are of a healthy body weight. Here I am with some of the girls, supporting the S0S (Stop 0 Size) campaign.

Me and one of my True Models, Victoria, promoting Just GTIs.

We work hard but we know how to have a party too!

Above: Bunny Girl Party.

Below left: True isn't just for the girls – here are a couple of my male models with Louisa Lytton, who played Ruby in *EastEnders*.

Below right: The flyer for one of our Christmas parties.

The knowledge that I am helping other BDD sufferers has really helped me through tough times – I've come a long way and I'm not about to give up now!
Inset: My dog, Peanut – she's one of the most important things in my life.

getting on, and she told them I was about to start a job and was doing a lot better. She wanted me to do the interview because she thought it would inspire people if I talked about the progress I'd made since the original article in the *Daily Mail*, and in the end she persuaded me.

When the woman from the *Sunday People* came down to interview me, I mentioned that I was about to start a job and that I had a boyfriend, and said, 'I'm finally starting to feel as though I'm coming out on the other side of the illness. The response I've had to the other newspaper articles and TV programmes has really helped, and I feel I'm 50 per cent there.'

Looking back, 50 per cent was probably rather over-optimistic, but it was what I thought at the time.

I thought the reporter wanted to hear all the positive things about the progress I'd made, so I began to feel really uncomfortable when she kept asking me questions like, 'And do you like being in your underwear around your boyfriend?'

Embarrassed and taken aback, I said, 'No. No, I don't. But I'm not like that anyway. It's not my nature, and I wouldn't be like that even if I was totally recovered.' But she didn't give up. Obviously she had an idea in her head of what she wanted to write and was determined to make me say something she could use. Eventually I gave up and said, 'I'm really sorry, but I can't give you what you want. I've only just got to the point when I let my boyfriend see me without lipstick, and I think that's quite an achievement.'

Mum had encouraged me to do the interview because the experience with the *Daily Mail* had been so positive – they'd written a really good article and I'd had such a good response from so many people that it had helped me too. So we were appalled when we saw what this woman had written in the *Sunday People*.

She did an awful story, 'quoting' me as having said things like, 'I used to think I was ugly, but now I love romping naked for my man.' It was dreadful, and I was absolutely shocked and humiliated. It had such a bad effect on me that, for the first time in many months, I cut myself and tried to strangle myself when I saw it. It was truly one of the worst moments of my life.

The reporter had a Dictaphone, so there was evidence that the words she used weren't my words – or anything like them. I know journalists might ask you questions that start with, 'Would you say that…?' and if you nod or say 'Yeah' they can use it as a quote. But I'd actually said 'No' in answer to her questions, and it was as though she'd just decided to lie.

The article she wrote really set me back, so Mum phoned her, very distressed, and said, 'You have no idea what you've done to Racheal.'

I wouldn't come out of my room and I was almost back at the beginning again as far as any recovery was concerned. I think Mum felt really awful about it, because she'd encouraged me to do the interview and so she felt responsible for what had happened. But how could she have had any idea that they'd do something like that – or that they'd want to, particularly to someone who was ill?

When Mum complained to the newspaper, they said they'd print a story to put the record straight, but I didn't want to be in their paper again under any circumstances, and I just couldn't go through with it. I didn't trust them and I'd had enough. But I did receive a lovely bunch of flowers from that woman. Thanks a lot!

I look back now and realise how naive I was at the time, but I was too upset to do anything about it. Having had that experience myself, I can understand why people don't want to pursue things when newspapers write lies about them. You just feel completely drained, and no retraction of the story in small print tucked away somewhere in the recesses of a newspaper is going to redress that balance.

In the past I hadn't wanted to do interviews because I felt

ashamed of who I was and didn't want the spotlight shining on me and on all my anxieties and insecurities. But that article in the *Sunday People* taught me a salutary lesson and reinforced the feelings of distrust in people outside my own family that I'd only just begun to overcome. It was very hard to trust anyone after that, so I started making sure that, if I did agree to be interviewed, they had to show me what they were going to print beforehand, so I could see how they'd worded things and check the article over. Unfortunately, they don't let you approve pictures, so I could never see the picture they were going to use until the article was printed, and that was always a nightmare. I'd already destroyed all my mum's snapshots of me by scratching out my face, and seeing my picture in an article always sent me back into depression.

Eventually, as I started to get over my disappointment at having to give up college, Paul said, 'I think you really need to get out of the house, Racheal. It doesn't matter if you don't have any qualifications. You can still get a job.'

I think he felt that Mum was feeding my disorder to some degree because she didn't push me out and make me cope. I know she was doing her best and that she was frightened to put too much pressure on me because she simply didn't know how I'd respond. But Paul's natural attitude was just to ignore things, and he felt that, if I went out there and jumped in at the deep end, maybe I'd come out swimming.

Mum must have agreed with him to some extent, although I think she didn't want to be the one to do the actual pushing. In her mind it was one thing to make me do television programmes, because that was intended to help me. But because I'd been bullied in town, she realised that if I was working locally I'd have to come face to face with local people, and she was afraid of what would happen if someone made a negative comment about me.

I wanted to please Paul, so I eventually typed up a CV, wrote a covering letter, which I illustrated liberally with drawings of daffodils, and then walked up the road, going into every shop and office and introducing myself and handing them a copy. It was a terrific achievement to have approached so many unknown people and I felt really good about having managed to do it – albeit after a lot of encouragement and pushing from my mum and, particularly, from Paul.

Unfortunately, though, nothing came of it and I didn't get any job offers immediately, which was disappointing but not really surprising, as I had no qualifications and no work experience. Also, because I felt so shy going into all these places, I probably came across as very nervous. But, although it made me feel rejected and that nobody wanted me, I did realise I'd made another small step forward.

Then, a little later, just before Christmas, I was offered a temporary job for a month working at a Virgin Megastore, with the promise that they'd keep me on if I did well. I was really proud of myself. But the reality of working was even more difficult than I'd anticipated. Although I worked really hard when I was there, I was still very ill and was calling in sick every other day. So, not surprisingly, they didn't take up the option of giving me a permanent job after my month's trial.

I was still taking five hours a day to get ready and was still obsessed about my skin, but I couldn't phone up Virgin and say, 'I can't come in today because of my face.' When I did go in, I was working behind the till – in full, unprotected, public view – which was really hard. One day I heard a girl in the queue say to her friend, 'Oh, God, look at that girl's eyebrows!' It felt as though something had clamped around my stomach and I thought I was going to be sick. Desperate to hide, I said I had to go to the loo, and locked myself in there and sobbed, thinking, 'What am I going to do? I can't go back out there.' But I eventually forced myself to calm down and somehow managed to get through the rest of the day.

Looking back on it now, I realise it was completely the wrong environment for me at the time, particularly working in a store in Crawley, because some of the people coming in were people who'd bullied me in town. It might have helped a bit if I'd felt comfortable with the people I was working with and hadn't tried to hide the fact that I had a problem. But at least I'd tried, and I was grateful that someone had wanted to employ me, particularly as Paul was on at me every day saying, 'You've got to get a job. Just get out there. Don't listen to your mum. You have to stand on your own two feet.'

Shortly afterwards, Paul's mum offered me a job in the shoe shop she worked at. Because she'd never really understood my illness, or my depression, she was always saying to my mum, 'Get that girl a job. Get her out of the house.' I knew Paul wanted me to do it, and I wanted to impress him, so I decided I'd do my best and give it a try. But it was awful. Most days I'd phone up saying I was ill and Paul's mum would go mad. Sometimes, when I did go in, I wouldn't want to be seen by the public and I'd sit in the staff room and refuse to come out. Obviously I wasn't a very good employee, and that caused a lot of problems between Paul and me. In fact, I barely went to that job, and one morning I woke up and said, 'Look, can you just phone your mum and tell her I can't come in any more? Tell her I'm not well,' which didn't go down too well because she didn't understand.

Paul had done a paper round from the age of 12 and I think his mum just thought I was ungrateful and that my mum was feeding my illness. She thought that offering me a job might help me gain some independence and stand on my own two feet, and for a normal teenager that would probably have been the right thing to do. But, unfortunately, being a BDD sufferer meant I wasn't a 'normal' teenager, and for me it only highlighted what a failure I was.

17

Working

Mum had joined the gym at a local health club called Esporta and one day she was chatting to one of the receptionists when she mentioned she'd really like me to get a job, and the receptionist said, 'Actually we're looking for someone to work on reception at the moment.' So Mum came home with an application form. Paul kept saying, 'Just fill it out, Racheal. Have a go. You can only try,' and in the end I agreed, if only to satisfy him and Mum. To my amazement, shortly afterwards I was asked to go for an interview, although I'm sure that my mum, being the chatterbox she is, somehow pushed them into it.

In fact, doing the television programmes had helped me a lot more than I realised, because they made me learn to switch from being me to being a person who talks, and I was able to use that ability in my interview. The interview was held in the beauty salon at the health club, which was a lovely environment, with dim lighting and soft music playing. Even so, I felt really nervous and shy and I don't know how I managed to force myself to open the door and walk through it. But as soon as I stepped over the threshold, I suddenly became this chatty person who was talking away and seemed absolutely fine, helped by the fact that Debs, the woman who interviewed me, was really easy to talk to. Then, as soon as I stepped outside the room again, I was back to being anxious, shy and insecure.

Of course, because of the depression I'd suffered from for the past few years, I didn't have any real work experience, so I'd had to exaggerate a bit on my CV, and there wasn't much I could say during the interview except that I was really keen to start working my way up the ladder in a company. So I was astonished to be offered the job. It was an extraordinary experience for me, as it was the first time I'd felt as though someone actually wanted me and that I finally had a purpose to my life. Although the prospect of working there was terrifying, I was elated at having done something difficult and succeeded, which was a feeling I couldn't remember having had for a very long time, if ever.

I don't think things would have worked out as well as they did if not for the fact that my manager, Debs, was a really lovely lady, very sympathetic, encouraging and supportive. I don't know if she had any prior knowledge of me, but I certainly felt as though she wanted to give me a chance. A colleague told me later that everyone thought I was really moody and miserable because I didn't talk to anyone and was always hiding under my hair, which they mistook for signs that I was stuck up. But I think Debs probably understood a great deal more than she let on, because she was very, very good with me. It was the fact that she put up with some things that a boss in any other job probably wouldn't have that helped me get to where I am today. She made sure there was plenty of structure in the day and used to give me little goals and incentives such as cinema tickets or chocolate bars for my achievements. She made me feel like somebody, and I think that's what I had been sorely lacking – that sense of purpose and of having a place in the world.

It was probably the hardest job I could have done at that stage of my illness, having to deal with everyone who came into the health club, and I did put tremendous pressure on myself about how I had to look. It took me five hours to get ready on the first day. Although I'd reached the point of being able to wear just mascara, eye shadow, blusher and foundation when I was with Paul or my parents, it still had to be full make-up for work. Unfortunately, there was a mirror right next to where I stood in reception, so I was constantly looking in it and reapplying my make-up (which I hid in a cupboard) when no one was looking. But, despite being really nervous, I did manage to smile at the club members.

To my surprise and enormous relief, I managed to get through that first shift and went home at the end of the day feeling a sense of achievement and of having done something constructive that I'd never felt before. I'd been out for the whole day and had had to interact with people all day long, and, although I'd felt like it several times, I hadn't walked out. I'd made it and I was so proud of myself. Although it had been really hard, I felt I'd missed out on so much at school that I desperately wanted to make a success of it. Perhaps even more than that, though, I really liked Debs and had told her in my interview how great I was going to be in the job, and I didn't want to let her down. Since I'd first started doing television and other interviews, I'd practised preparing myself for interactions with other people by taking a deep breath and thinking, Lights! Camera! Action! It was a technique I'd finally become able to switch on at will. I'd used it in my interview at Esporta and I was determined to make Debs proud of me by turning the pretence into a reality.

Some of my shifts started at six o'clock in the morning, and to begin with I had to get up at 1am to have enough time to apply my make-up and get ready. I don't know what I was doing for all those hours, but that's how long it took me. So, if I had an early shift, I'd have to go to bed at about six in the evening. The most difficult times were when I'd have a late shift and an early shift back to back – I'd work until eleven at night and then have to start at six the next morning – and on those nights I wouldn't get any sleep at all. So, inevitably I became absolutely exhausted, although in a way that was good because, as I was either at work or asleep, I didn't have time to think too much and to dwell on things. Fortunately, Debs was quite flexible about people swapping their shifts, and that's what I'd try to do whenever I could, giving some excuse like 'It's my brother's birthday'. But there's only a certain number of times you can do that before people start saying, 'No. That's enough. People don't always want to be working your late shifts.'

After I'd been at Esporta for about six months, it gradually began to dawn on me that people seemed to like me for who I was. Members would come into the club and ask for me by name, and after all the bullying – which I'd always thought I deserved – and everything else I'd been through, it was an amazing feeling to know that these people wanted to know me. For the first time I felt accepted by people other than my family. I knew my family would always accept me, no matter what, but the people at work didn't have to, and so it was a really nice feeling. I began to be comfortable at work and to trust the people I worked with and the regular club members I saw all the time – and I began to realise that what I looked like was unimportant.

Eventually, because I was getting so little sleep, I began to get run down and had a constant cold. Also, the hours I was spending getting ready each day became ridiculous and I knew I was going to have to start reducing the amount of make-up I wore. I'd always worn my hair down, like a curtain over my face, so first I decided to save a bit of time getting ready by going to work with my hair in a ponytail. To most people that would seem too insignificant to mention, but for someone with BDD it was a massive step to take — to tie my hair back and let people see my face.

The first time I did it, I felt awful about myself on the way to work, and Paul kept trying to reassure me as I repeatedly checked my reflection in the mirror above the passenger seat in his car. To my amazement, when I arrived at work everyone said, 'Oh, we really like it. You look lovely with your hair up,' and that evening Paul told me, 'If you'd looked like that when I first saw you, I'd have been too scared to approach you. You look so pretty with your hair back.' But I still thought people were having a laugh at my expense, because I simply couldn't believe what they seemed to be saying — that they liked my face.

The next step was to stop wearing eyeliner, and in time I reached the point of being able to go to work wearing just the make-up I'd previously only allowed my family to see me with. I managed to convince myself that, as long as I wore mascara, foundation, blusher and lip gloss, I'd have covered all the essential parts of my face that needed hiding. I still had to put layers and layers of foundation on, which for me at that time was 'hardly any make-up', but now it was only taking me two hours to get ready. (In fact, I've since discovered that I'm allergic to all foundation and can no longer use it, so presumably I was causing the skin problems that made me so miserable.) It was a huge step forward, but that's not to say that it marked an end to all my bizarre behaviour. For example, if I wanted to draw attention away from my face at any time, I'd dampen tiny pieces of tissue paper and stick them all over. People must have thought I was very strange, although no one really said anything.

The most extraordinary part of it all for me was that people still seemed to like me and still wanted to know me, and I was nominated by the club members for the 'Top Banana' award, which meant winning a £50 bonus and having a little plaque put up on the wall in reception. And that's when I finally started to come out of myself. I'd spent so long feeling bitter and angry about how I looked and how nasty I was as a person that it took me a while to recognise the fact that I was starting to like who I was.

If depression threatened to overwhelm me as I was going into work, instead of having a BDD attack I'd think, 'Right. Deep breath. Just face it.' And I did; I faced it all day, day after day, and it got better and better, until I began to be the sort of person I wanted to be. I finally accepted the fact that I couldn't really change what I looked like, but that that didn't matter if people were happy to accept me for who I was – and that felt really, really good.

I worked in reception at Esporta for two years, by which time I'd reduced the amount of make-up I wore so much that I was able to go to work wearing only mascara. But it never ceased to surprise me when people complimented me and said, 'Oh, you look so much prettier than you did when you used to wear all that make-up.'

Then one day Debs told me that they wanted to promote me and put me in sales. Although I was really pleased in one way, it was a daunting prospect because people's first impressions of the club would be affected by how I presented myself. If you walked into any sales department and saw someone who was really scruffy, it would colour your perception about whatever they were selling. So I knew that having to look the part would be an added pressure on me.

The interview for the sales job was with a different manager, so I was really scared and felt sure I'd come across as very nervous. When I went to see Debs afterwards, I told her I thought I'd messed it up. 'Well, Racheal,' she said, 'do you want to see the notes she wrote about you?' And, to my amazement, they were really good. I was over the moon and couldn't believe it when I read that I was 'quietly confident', when in truth I'd been shaking with terror. I still see myself as a really shy person, although people say I'm not, and so perhaps I've changed without realising it; I think that if you pretend long enough, you eventually become the person you're pretending to be. So perhaps I did well in my first interview at Esporta because I was acting the part of a 'quietly confident' person and maybe by this time that was who I really was.

However, working in sales meant that, rather than being with the people I'd learned to feel comfortable with, I was meeting new people – prospective club members – all the time. On reception I'd reached the point of being so tired that I didn't even wear lipstick, but I always wore it in sales and gradually started to increase the amount of other make-up I wore too, which was a reflection of my increased anxiety. In fact, all the different stages of my life are marked by the quantity and type of make-up I wore, which is fairly crazy. But this time it wasn't really driven by a fear of being judged, but more because I wanted to look a bit neater and tidier. I also bought some new suits, which I really enjoyed wearing because they made me feel good about myself, and that was a completely new feeling for me.

Of course, it was never going to be all plain sailing and sometimes I'd have a bad day and wouldn't want to see anybody, and I'd be really worried about who was going to come through the door whenever the receptionist told me there was a customer. I'd be frightened that it might be someone who'd bullied me and I'd have to concentrate really hard on thinking, 'Take a deep breath. Lights! Camera! Action!' In fact, there were times when some of the bullies I'd come across in town did come in and I'd have to shake their hands and smile and say, 'Hi,' and they'd just pretend they didn't recognise me. The first time it happened was when two girls who'd bullied me for a long, long time came in to look around. I think they worked as Virgin air hostesses and you could tell they were still quite bitchy. But I thought, 'I don't care what you think of me. I'm going to smile and shake your hands and take your membership money.' In the event it was fine: they didn't say anything and I think they joined.

I think sometimes the bullies were embarrassed, because I was in a position of authority in that it was my job to work out the rate they would have to pay for their membership, so they didn't want to annoy me!

Working at Esporta helped me to take a huge step forward in my recovery from BDD because, although I was still shy behind the door, it made me develop the ability to walk out of the office confidently, and by the time I was selling I had become that confident person.

But, having said that, I still wasn't at ease with myself, and I still had BDD attacks, although they didn't stop me working and I no longer ever reached the point of blacking out and self-harming. I'd sometimes throw ornaments and break things in a fit of anger and frustration, and I sometimes hated what I looked like. So it wasn't all rosy. But I wouldn't beat myself up and I was able to think, 'I'm not going to let it hold me back. I'm going to go to work and just get on with it.' There were a few times when I had to pretend I wasn't well because I desperately wanted to go home, but it was literally a handful of times during four years of working there.

Although I was still ill, and obviously hadn't made a complete recovery, I was managing better than I'd ever have thought possible. I'd come a long way from the worst days of my illness, but I still did some strange things at work. For example, we used to take it in turns to go to the bowling alley in the nearby leisure complex to buy sweets, and one day Simon, one of my colleagues, asked me if I'd go. Horrified, I said, 'No, I'm sorry. I can't.'

He was a bit surprised and said, 'Don't be stupid, Racheal. We're always buying the sweets. Don't be selfish.'

He didn't understand that I couldn't physically go, so I tried to explain by saying, 'Simon, I just can't be seen in the daylight today.' At Esporta the lighting was very good from my point of view, being quite dark, but I simply couldn't go out to the bowling alley, and I felt so panicked that I threw a tantrum and started crying. I think Simon was very taken aback at my reaction, which I suppose indicates how well I could hide my illness from people by that stage.

In fact, as soon as I moved into sales, I took out the light bulb above my desk and would sit in the corner of the office in the dark. Then one day the general manager came down and replaced all the dead and missing light bulbs, including mine. When I came into the office afterwards, I burst out crying, demanded to know why there was a light bulb above my desk, grabbed some balloons that were hanging in the office and hung them on the light fitting.

Looking somewhat bemused, the general manager said, 'Don't be stupid, Racheal. You can't do that. They're going to burst!'

I started crying and screaming, 'If you make me sit under that light bulb, I'm going to leave. I can't stay here. I'm going home,' and in the end he let me take the light bulb out. Although I don't suppose he understood why, I think he realised it was a huge issue for me and that that was the only way I could carry on working in the office.

A while later, when I was having a particularly bad day, even facing the light in the centre of the room became too much for me, and I turned my desk round so that it faced the wall. I'd find little strategies like that to enable me to cope, but I don't know how I managed to move between all that going on behind the scenes and talking to customers.

Inevitably, if I was having a bad day, I'd sometimes give away leads and lose out on sales. I wouldn't make it obvious, but when the receptionist came in to say there was someone to see me, I'd tell Simon or Matt or one of my other colleagues, 'It's all right.

You see them. I've got a lot of calls to make and I'm too busy.'

I don't know how I got away with behaviour like that, but I suspect some of the people there secretly already knew about my illness from the documentaries I'd been in. Otherwise they couldn't have understood my occasionally odd behaviour and wouldn't have put up with it. In fact, although I didn't know until much later, Malcolm, my general manager, had read my story in the *Daily Mail*, when I was so ill. So I think they may have given me the job initially because they were trying to give me a chance. But, whatever the background to it all, the people at Esporta became my 'safe' people, like my family, and I have a great deal to be thankful to them for.

It was the best place I could have worked, because I saw the same members every day and was able to get used to them, and because I was surrounded by people who were used to taking care of their appearance. So it was a really nice environment for me, and possibly the only one in which I could have coped at that stage of my illness.

There were also lots of people at Esporta who were individually helpful as a result of their attitudes towards me. For example, there was a girl called Laura – who's a good friend of mine now – and, although she was only 17 at the time, she was really understanding. I'd arrive at work and she'd say, 'Are you all right? If you're having a bad day, I can tell people you're busy,' and she'd say to them, 'I'm sorry, but Racheal has appointments all day today and I'm afraid you can't see her.' She really looked after me in that way, and, although it obviously might not have been very good from a business point of view, I think I made enough sales for them to put up with that from time to time.

The only negative thing about working at Esporta was that my eating disorder probably reached its worst point while I was there. I wouldn't eat anything at all while I was at work except for one Ricicle (a little square of marshmallow and Rice Krispies), which

I think has about 120 calories. So inevitably I sometimes felt dizzy and faint. I was doing extremely well with extracting the make-up, but that meant that the only thing I felt I was still in control of was my weight, and I hadn't really associated that with BDD. The more weight I lost, the better I felt. It sounds silly but if I'd eaten something, I'd feel really big and wouldn't have the confidence to make the sales.

Although I'm five feet eight and weighed only six stone, I was convinced I was fat, and had no idea that in fact I was ridiculously skinny – although perhaps that wouldn't be considered 'skinny' these days when 'size 0' seems to be so popular. It was only recently, when I found some photos from around that time, that I realised how shockingly emaciated I really looked. It got to the point where my colleagues started to comment on it, and they were very concerned about my eating habits. People would say to me, 'You really do need to put on some weight, Racheal,' and one of the ladies would always make sure there was coffee and a biscuit waiting for me on my table in the mornings.

So, although the BDD was improving, it wasn't until a very long time later that I overcame the eating disorder.

I don't have any photographs that were taken when I was really ill. Mum used to try to make me pose for pictures in the hope that I'd see how nice I looked, but whenever I saw one I'd be really upset and say, 'It's awful. Why would you do this to me? Why are you making me have to confront what a freak I am?' Poor Mum was always trying to make me see what she saw, but it wasn't ever going to happen – it just doesn't with this illness. But that was another positive aspect of working at Esporta, because as I grew in confidence I eventually became a bit more comfortable about being photographed.

Basically I owe everything to that job, because it really did bring me out of myself and make me face my fear. Although the BDD didn't go away, working at Esporta opened up for me the possibility that I might be able to succeed at something, and it gave me the drive to go on and do other things I'd never previously have thought I could do. It did a massive amount to build up my confidence. When I went from reception into sales, I had a 98 per cent closing rate on new club memberships and the second-best sales among the 60 clubs in the region. So I was really proud of myself. Most of the women who went there were lovely; they'd tell me what a great representative I was for the club and how well presented I always was, and some of them would say, 'I'd never have joined if it hadn't been for you, Racheal,' which made me feel really good about myself – for the first time in my life.

Some of the customers knew I was suffering from BDD and I think they felt more comfortable talking to me about weight issues than they might have done talking to someone who probably wouldn't have understood them so well. You can't go through an illness like BDD and not come out of it with a better understanding of other people and their body-image problems. So I knew what I was talking about, and I was a good listener, and I think people trusted me and felt I'd do my best to make sure they were looked after, which I did. And feeling that I had the respect of people at Esporta gave me a tremendous boost. They were a fantastic team of really lovely people.

Just before I moved into sales, at a time when I was enjoying myself and feeling better than I could ever remember feeling before, Paul and I rented a one-bedroom flat and moved in together, and I started to feel I was independent for the first time. Your mum and dad always want to look after you, and I think Paul felt I needed to be taken out of my parents' grasp and be pushed in at the deep end – which was a risky idea that fortunately worked. Paul and I each paid half the rent, so once we had the flat I had to work and couldn't afford to be sacked, because I needed to have regular money coming in. So, although that was another pressure, it was also an added incentive to make me keep going. It must be the same sort of feeling people experience when they have children: they can no longer afford to let themselves go under, however bad they may feel. For the first time I had responsibilities and commitments that I couldn't just walk away from each time I wasn't feeling too good.

After I'd been at Esporta for about four years, the club started going downhill a bit. The funding was reduced and they stopped repairing or replacing things when they broke, and also increased the membership fee quite substantially. That was a particular problem for me, because I have to believe in what I'm selling and I didn't think it was good value for money any more. The management changed at around the same time, and they gradually started to make people redundant, including a lot of the people I'd become close to and loved and trusted. Some of them were replaced with new people and it felt as though my safe little environment was being invaded. The business was sold to Virgin shortly afterwards, so perhaps they were allowing it to run down a bit before the sale.

We were then told we had to sell from a script, which I didn't believe in. I'd earn a commission on the memberships I sold, but it wasn't just 'sales' to me; it was never about the money, but about the satisfaction of making people feel good about themselves. It was a fantastic feeling when people came in to show me how much weight they'd lost and to say thank you. That's a greater reward than any amount of money.

Gradually the members started getting upset because of the deterioration in the club's facilities, and I felt as though I was responsible in some way, as though I was letting people down. In the four years I'd been at Esporta I'd done so much and made more progress than I'd ever thought possible, but I suppose nothing lasts for ever and there comes a time to move on, and it felt as though fate was giving me a push.

One of the members at the club owned an estate agency, and

he asked me if I'd like to go and work for him. The unimaginable had happened: I'd been headhunted! So I started working in his office, but the hours were long – I often worked from seven in the morning untill ten at night. As we weren't allowed to keep anything on our desks and didn't have any drawers, there was nowhere for me to hide my secret stash of make-up and mirror. So I just found it a bit too much, particularly having moved from what was a very safe and unthreatening environment at Esporta.

I'd agreed to work at the estate agency because I knew the member concerned quite well and felt I could trust him and feel comfortable. But I hadn't realised quite how strict he was as a boss and how dedicated he was to the work – which is a good thing, of course, but it was too much for me at that time. I also really missed Esporta and ended up going back there to my old job in sales. But I found it really difficult. It was another lesson learned, I suppose: going back in life is often a mistake, because things move on in your absence.

They'd introduced the scripts, which I hated, and they wanted me to wear a uniform. All the members used to tell me they loved the way I dressed and they'd comment on how smart I looked, which made me even more keen to make the effort. But the big issue to me was that I felt as though they were trying to make us 'numbers' rather than allowing us to be individuals. The fact that I'd been known as a person, with value in my own right, had made me feel really good, and I was quite strongly against the idea of being 'depersonalised'.

So, after a couple of months, I went in to see Malcolm, the general manager, and told him, 'I'm going to have to leave for good now. I just don't feel as though I can take all these changes on board. My closing rate is 98 per cent. That means that only 2 per cent of people who come in and see me don't join. How can I improve on that?' I really didn't think a script could increase my sales ratio, because I believe the most important aspect of selling is people feeling they can relate to you, otherwise you just appear really boring and insincere.

Malcolm said, 'I'd beg you to stay, Racheal, but I'm going to hand in my notice tomorrow too.'

So we both left, and it was shortly afterwards that the club was sold.

After I left Esporta I was talking to my brother James one day when he asked if I'd like to work for him. He has a company called Just GTIs, which is a car dealership where he and his team restore Peugeot 205 GTIs back to classic cars, which were always his childhood passion. Accepting that job turned out to be another very significant turning point for me.

James gave me some overalls and explained that my job was essentially to remove all the modified parts from the cars and put them on eBay, as well as organising the office and getting all the accounts sorted out, which he didn't have time to do himself. I introduced some more structure into the place, but it wasn't enough to fill the days, so I also became involved in all the dirty stuff, which I absolutely loved. After working at Esporta, where I had to be really well presented, I loved getting my hands dirty and spending my time doing something completely different.

Although I was still wearing make-up when I started working at Just GTIs, I gradually reduced it until I ended wearing none at all. I was cleaning up filthy car parts every day and getting covered in oil, and I realised that all that on top of my foundation probably wasn't doing my skin much good. By that time I'd become so comfortable with who I was that make-up didn't matter any more, and everyone was so nice to me that I didn't feel they were judging me at all.

While I was working at Just GTIs, my mum went to college to do a web design course and one day she showed me the basics of what she'd learned. As I'm quite creative and have always loved art and designing clothes, I found web design hugely enjoyable. So, when my brother told me he wanted a new website for his business, I bought a book and played around with lots of ideas until I got quite good at it and was able to redesign and improve his website for him. Web design is still something I do for people to this day and it continues to give me an enormous amount of pleasure and provides an outlet for my creative side.

So a whole new world was opening up to me, one in which I was finding things I enjoyed doing and, to my amazement, was apparently good at. It was a strange and exciting feeling for someone who'd spent so many years convinced she was worthless and had no right to a place in the world like other people.

18

A Holiday in The Sun

While I was working at Esporta, I went on holiday to Cyprus with my brothers James and Jason and their respective wife and girlfriend, Emma and Anna. Being quite a lot older than me, my brothers hadn't spent much time at home while I was at my most ill, so although I was already on the road to recovery by this time – with the exception of the eating disorder, which I still had – they were really shocked by my behaviour.

I agreed to go with them because I thought it would help to clear up my (imaginary) skin problems. But it was hard, because, as much as I love the sun, I hate the light that comes with it. So it was a vicious circle and there were days when I refused to leave my room, or would get to the beach and catch sight of my reflection, think my skin was getting bad and scurry back to the hotel to hide myself away.

At that time I didn't realise how distressed my brothers were by my behaviour, but apparently James phoned Mum in tears and said, 'What's wrong with Racheal? I never realised she was this bad.'

Also, as I began to tan, the scars on my arms became more obvious, and my brothers were totally shocked when they saw them, as they had no idea I'd been self-harming. Of course, from Mum's point of view I was considerably better than I had been and had come a long way since the early days of my illness, so she was rather surprised when James was so troubled by my behaviour. God only knows how my brothers would have reacted if they'd seen me when I was inhaling the aerosols and all the rest of it.

The funny thing was that in my own head I was already halfway down the road to recovery, because I was working and coping with the job better than I'd ever imagined possible. But obviously to my brothers my behaviour was quite a shock and they were really upset by it. They'd seen me refuse point-blank to go out, and they were used to my dad being a bit like that too, so the signs of my illness they'd witnessed at home hadn't seemed too extreme to them.

One day I'd been shut away in my hotel room since morning when James knocked on the door to tell me we were all going out for dinner. But I said, 'I'm not coming out today,' and refused to open the door. When I felt like that, there was nothing that would persuade me to go out. James kept saying, 'Racheal, would you *please* just open the door?' and I finally burst into tears and begged him to go away and leave me alone.

That was a rather bizarre aspect of my recovery: one day I could go out to the beach and another I couldn't even bear to be seen. So some days I obviously felt OK, although I used to wear full make-up even on the beach, which wouldn't have helped my skin at all and probably brought on a flare-up of spots, and that may have been the reason I stopped wanting to leave my room towards the end of the holiday. But I didn't realise all of that then.

During that holiday I wouldn't eat a thing, although I didn't know my brothers had noticed and I had no idea they were so worried about me. As I was very skinny, they were really concerned about the health issues that would arise if I continued to starve myself. But they didn't want me to feel like a freak, or to know how worried they were about me, so they left me to it and didn't put any pressure on me to come out of my room if I didn't want to.

However, there was one occasion when I was in my room with Emma and Anna and they were trying to make me go with them to dinner. They assured me I was thin and told me to stand next to them and look in the mirror in the hope that I'd compare myself to their size-8 figures and realise I wasn't fat. But while I saw them both as perfect, I thought I looked five times larger. Eventually Emma became very frustrated and said, 'Come on! You must be able to see how thin you are, Racheal.' But I honestly couldn't. I saw myself as huge and disfigured and there was nothing anyone could say that would change that. Then Emma asked me to explain what I saw and I grabbed my 'fat' legs and said, 'Look! It's obvious.' Realising there was no getting through to me, they left my room to go down to dinner and I sat on the bed and cried, feeling very confused and wishing I could see what they claimed they saw. But that was never going to happen, because the more I looked at myself, the worse I felt. Eventually, miserable and disappointed, I decided to go to bed in the hope that I'd dream of eating a tasty feast without any feelings of guilt.

Looking back on it now, I think my brothers may have decided to take me away on that holiday to give me a break, because I always blamed Mum for everything at that time, and so they must have thought she was putting too much pressure on me. They'd seen me getting upset when Mum forced me to do television programmes and they'd get angry with her. But I don't think they realised I'd reached such a low point that the only way was up, and although I did get worse before I got better, Mum's tactic had worked.

I was very pleased with myself for going on holiday, and thought I was doing really well – making it to the beach in daylight was quite a significant step forward for me. But I think it was that holiday that made my brothers finally understand what everyone else had been putting up with and just how ill I was. Although they were at home when the illness first started, I think they assumed it was all to do with Fay's death, and finding that I was still acting like that ten years later really scared them.

19

A Tragic Death and a Sudden Realisation

It was while I was working at Just GTIs that my friend Ethan died. Ethan was a club member at Esporta, which is where I'd met him, and I'd got to know him very well. He was one of those people who enjoy living on the edge, and he was a really sweet boy. I say 'boy', but in fact he was 27 when I was 22. He was very good to me and would always pick me up and drop me at home if I was out of town and couldn't get hold of Paul to come and collect me.

James and I were having a really lovely day at Hampton Court when my friend Belinda rang to say that Ethan had had a skydiving accident and was in hospital. All she knew was that he'd apparently attempted to turn and didn't make it. We didn't receive any other news for hours, but eventually my phone rang again and I almost cried with relief when Ethan's number came up on the screen. But it was a relief that was to be short-lived, as it wasn't Ethan but his sister, who said simply, 'He's dead.'

It was too much of a shock to take in and I couldn't believe that something so tragic could happen when things were just starting to work out for him. He used to tell me that he had a feeling he was going to die before he was 28, which I took as just one of those things people say sometimes, and I'd tell him not to be so silly. But to him it was a conviction and it was part of the reason he was so anxious to settle down, and why I'd been so delighted when he told me a couple of days before his death that he felt ready to move on. He'd sold his house, paid off all his credit cards and for the past two months had had a lovely girlfriend and was really happy.

When Fay died, I just wanted to die too, so that I could be with her, but I hadn't been as close as that to Ethan – he was my friend, whereas Fay had been more like a sister. So Ethan's death affected me in a different way, but it was a terrible tragedy and it made everything seem so pointless. He'd managed to turn his life around and was heading in a positive direction, with so much to look forward to, and suddenly he was dead.

The immediate pain of losing him was accompanied by an overwhelming feeling of guilt. How could I have been so selfish? How could I have wasted so much time in my life? I'd been ill for so many years, reduced to a shadow of a person by what I perceived as other people's opinions of me, people who didn't even matter. I know now that my illness was something I had no control over at the time and that beating myself up about it served no useful purpose. But the tragedy of Ethan's death made me take a fresh look at myself and forced me to realise how important it is not to waste whatever time we have in agonising about things that don't really matter. The day had arrived to make a fresh start and to make the most of every opportunity and learn to deal with everything life might throw at me.

Although I was working at Just GTIs and had made huge steps forward on the road to recovery, I was still missing out on so many opportunities. There was so much more I could be doing, but I'd been holding myself back because I never really felt comfortable in my own skin. I was avoiding doing all the things a lot of people take for granted, such as going out with my friends and just enjoying life, and, at 22, I'd become pretty much 'married', hidden and invisible and reluctant to leave my comfort zone.

Fay and Ethan were gone, but we're all going to die some time and people living 100 years from now won't even be aware that we ever existed. So it's up to us to make the best of what we've got while we've got it, because, like Ethan, none of us knows what's around the next corner in our lives.

The day after Ethan died, I was sitting at the computer looking through his pictures on MSN Messenger when an email popped up from 'Miss England', which said words to the effect of: 'Hello, Rebecca. You've made it through to the finals of Miss England. Congratulations!' Irritated and feeling that my grief had been intruded on by someone's foolish mistake, I emailed back: 'I'm sorry. My name's not Rebecca. I think you have the wrong person.' But within a few moments I received a reply: 'Sorry to have called you Rebecca. But you are the right person, Racheal.'

Still convinced it was at best a mistake and at worst a joke, I phoned my mum and asked if she knew what was going on. 'Oooh,' she said with undisguised delight. 'You've got through to the finals!'

'Mum, what have you done?' I asked nervously.

'Well, I feel you've missed out on so much, so I sent in some photos,' she answered.

When I left Esporta and was working at Just GTIs, I was wearing overalls all the time and so had a lot of clothes I didn't need any more, which I'd been selling off on eBay to make some extra money. Having found they sold better if they were advertised with accompanying pictures of someone wearing them, Mum had taken some photos of me in the shirts and various other items and I'd managed to sell quite a few things. Unknown to me, Mum had then sent in some of these pictures –

awful amateur photographs – to enter me in the Miss England competition. They pick about five girls from photographic entries and I'd been selected to enter the finals as Miss Crawley.

On one of the rare occasions I'd gone out with Mum to the shops when I was 16 and very ill, I'd been approached by someone from the agency Models 1 who asked if I'd be interested in modelling. Of course, she was asking the wrong person. But, as I explained to Mum afterwards, they wouldn't have wanted me when they'd seen me without my long coat and could see what I really looked like and how fat I was.

I'd also had modelling offers after the article had been published in the *Daily Mail*, but I'd turned them all down without even thinking about them. But Mum had decided she wasn't going to let me waste any more opportunities. When she was young she turned down the photographer David Bailey when he asked to photograph her – a decision she'd always regretted – so she was determined I wasn't going to have the same regrets and, when it was too late, think, 'I could have done so much.' Apparently, she'd read about the Miss England competition in a magazine and had decided she'd just see if I was accepted, and battle it out with me later.

Although I was horrified by the suggestion to begin with, the fact that it had come up on the day after Ethan's death, when I was looking as his pictures, made me realise how proud he'd have been of me if I could put myself in a situation in which everyone would be judging me on my looks. It was like fate. I felt that everyone had judged me throughout my entire life and I suddenly decided, well, let them. I'd be facing my greatest fear and, if I could do that, I knew no one could ever make me feel bad about myself again. Because I'd already been thinking about the fragility of life following Ethan's death, I thought, 'I could die tomorrow. So why not give it a go and do something that contradicts everything I've ever done throughout my life so far. It's time to see if I can really make a fresh start.'

It was a huge step from what had seemed to me to be the quite significant achievement of being able to go to work without make-up and be happy just wearing overalls, but perhaps it was a step I was ready to take – although in retrospect I don't think I was quite as ready as I thought at the time. And it was then that I suddenly realised something about myself: I like to be given opportunities and then turn them down; I think it gives me some sort of reassurance. I'd once gone with Mum to the Clothes Show, where I'd been given a card by the model agency Select, and, although I was really pleased they thought I might be of interest to them, I had no intention of pursuing the offer. It was the same thing with Miss England: I was honoured to know they wanted me, but I didn't really want to do it. But what *was* different this time was that I decided to force myself to see it through.

When I was a little girl, Mum used to watch Miss World every year, so I'd grown up being aware of beauty pageants and had enjoyed watching them with her. Suddenly this seemed the perfect opportunity to repay people for all the pain I'd put them through over the years. All I'd ever done was hurt my mum, and the perfect reward for all her patience and belief in me would be to do something positive to show everyone I'd overcome my illness, so that they could be proud of me instead of worried about me. It also seemed to be a wonderful chance to gather all the family together to witness me face my fear and conquer it once and for all. So that there didn't seem to be much option other than to go ahead with it and try to break the pattern I'd built up over years of running away when the going got tough.

20

Miss England 2004

When I arrived at the Miss England competition, I realised immediately that it wasn't going to be as easy as I'd thought. I'd put a lot of pressure on myself in the run-up to it because I'd started to feel that some kind of cruel joke was being played on me, and the words 'Why would they want me?' kept running through my head. I'd reached the point of accepting myself because of the work I'd done and the fact that people seemed to like me for who I was and weren't bothered by what I looked like, and I was leading an almost normal life and had started to feel comfortable inside my own skin. But now I was deliberately putting myself forward to be judged almost solely in terms of my looks again. However, I decided to take myself in hand and to remind myself that I'd learned not to care any more about what I looked like, but to concentrate instead on the person I was inside.

I think Mum wanted to make me see that what I was on the inside was reflected on the outside, to enable me to become complete, and she hoped I might somehow be shocked into realising that perhaps I wasn't so bad after all. In the end it didn't really do that, but it did give me more confidence and make me see that I *could* achieve things if I set my mind to them.

In the lead-up to the Miss England final, I did become quite anxious. I was repeatedly analysing my skin and worrying that it would flare up just in time for the competition, so much so that in the end my excessive picking at it created a problem and it did indeed become a mess. But I still pushed myself to take part, because for me it was about the fear I had to face rather than what I looked like.

I'd also already started to have serious doubts about my right to a place in the competition after a picture had been published in *Closer* magazine. With Miss England imminent, they'd done an article about what I'd been through and how I'd recovered and, using their own make-up artist, had also done a big photo shoot. At the time it all seemed great, but when the picture came out I thought, 'If that's the best they can make me look, I might as well pack up. What am I doing?' I felt really embarrassed because I was sure people would look at that picture and wonder why I was bothering to enter Miss England; they'd think that if I looked like that, I must still be ill. My mum tried to reassure me that the picture wasn't as awful as I thought and that it just didn't look like me – so at least that made me realise I can believe her when she does say a picture's good. I had to remind myself that I wasn't doing Miss England because of what I looked like, and fortunately I had enough strength by that time to keep going. Not long before that, a picture like the one in *Closer* would have had me reaching for an overdose, which shows just how far I'd come in my recovery by that time.

When I arrived at the hotel, The *Daily Mail* had got in touch when they heard I was entering the Miss England competition and had done a follow-up article to the one they'd published when I was ill. They of all people knew how ill I'd been, so they were really proud of me and felt that my story might be inspiring to other people. I was immediately plunged in among a noisy and excited group of girls of all different shapes and sizes. It was impossible not to be affected by the buzz in the atmosphere, and my own excitement started to grow. But I still had my doubts about it all, so I told the organiser, Angie, 'I'm really nervous because I don't feel I'm at the same level as the other girls in the competition and I don't really understand why you want me here.'

She looked at me in genuine surprise and said, 'Don't be mad, Racheal! Don't you know you're the favourite to win at the bookies?' At first I thought she was joking, but then put it down to the fact that people probably knew who I was as a result of the media attention I'd received in relation to BDD. It would make sense that they were backing me because of the good I try to do and because they probably thought I could do a lot more good if I had a title like 'Miss England'.

Angie was really kind and helped me to feel better about it all, but I think being the bookies' favourite definitely had its downside in that it made some of the girls see me as a threat. There were some absolutely gorgeous girls there, both physically and because of their personalities. Some of them knew about my illness and came over to me when I arrived and said, 'Oh my God! I've followed your story since you were young. You're so brave. Well done for being here.' One girl told me she'd been badly bullied but that my story had inspired her and was the reason she was there that day.

One thing I learned from that experience, to my surprise, is that a large percentage of the girls taking part in competitions like that were very insecure at school, with the result that they're constantly trying to seek approval for their appearance. Other girls are desperately trying to gain some sort of validation or approval from their parents. Although the other girls' problems were different from mine in many ways, they were also similar in that they never really feel good enough. So most of them aren't bitchy, as people might expect them to be, although there are some who fit that stereotype.

I hadn't come across Danielle Lloyd before, but I knew about her, and I noticed she clocked me immediately. She'd already taken part in lots of beauty pageants and had an air about her a bit like the American beauty queens who are more or less bred for it. She'd already won the UK equivalent of Miss Hawaiian Tropic, which is quite a difficult competition to do. In fact, I was asked to take part in it a couple of years later, but turned it down because it's quite raunchy, and you have to be confident and secure enough to be seen in your underwear by all the guys who are there.

After that article appeared, there was a story in another paper about how Danielle had been beaten up and how she used to wish she was ugly (a word I hate) so that people wouldn't look at her, and I was struck by the similarity of some of her expressions to the ones I'd used. She also said that her boyfriend had attacked her the day before the Miss Hawaiian Tropic final, and that she'd been run over by a car.

I can see that it might have appeared contradictory to some people that I'd had BDD and now I was doing the Miss England competition, but I was surprised at Danielle's story because she'd already done about 20 beauty pageants, including winning Miss Merseyside, and I wondered why she hadn't mentioned it all before. But you can never really understand why people do the things they do – as I should know, of all people – and it wasn't for me to judge. I didn't care about it at the time and I didn't see it as a bad thing; I just thought, 'Oh, you poor thing.'

I'd already been in email contact with some of the other

girls because it makes you feel more comfortable if you 'know' some of them before you get there, and I'd looked Danielle up on the Internet after reading the article, just to see who the competition was. So I felt sorry for her and made a point of smiling at her when I walked into the room for the rehearsals. But she just looked me up and down slowly as though I was a piece of crap. I felt really uncomfortable, because I was already convinced I shouldn't be there, and here was this girl who'd done about 20 competitions and had seen hundreds of beautiful girls and she obviously shared my opinion. But all I could do was try to ignore my discomfort and concentrate on the rehearsal.

Being a girl who was once absolutely terrified at the thought of having to stand up in class and read from a book, walking in front of the other girls was a really big thing for me, and that was when my experience at Esporta came into play. When I worked in sales, I had to sell corporate memberships as well as individual ones, which meant having to go to businesses and stand in front of up to 300 people and sell the club to them, and that was when I learned, with the help of my colleagues and manager, to block out the audience. Without that, I don't think I'd have been able to switch off and cope with doing Miss England.

But I was still nervous. When you don't feel good about yourself, being surrounded by beautiful girls is guaranteed to make you feel even worse, and I became more and more convinced I'd been included in the finals of the competition as a publicity stunt. I thought that, because I'd been in the newspaper and people knew about my illness and were sympathetic towards me, the competition organisers had decided to include me for the media attention it might attract. So I had to keep reminding myself that it didn't really matter, because I wasn't there to win; I was just there to prove something to myself. I didn't care if I came last as long as I faced my fear and showed my family I could do it. But, even so, you don't want people looking at you as if you're some kind of freak.

It was the first time I'd ever done any catwalk work, so my walk wasn't at all like the other girls' and I had to keep practising, and out of the corner of my eye I could see Danielle and her friends laughing. By the time I did Miss England, I'd come a long way since the bad days, but I suddenly felt again like I did when I was at school and I desperately wanted to run away and hide. Then I thought, 'No, Racheal. You've put yourself up for this. What did you expect? You knew you were going to be in a situation where you'd be judged on your looks again. Just go with it.' So I tried my best to block it out and carry on.

The rehearsals started quite early in the morning, at about eight o'clock, and at midday we went for lunch. I was standing in a group of really lovely girls I got on well with, eating our bits of lettuce and complaining about how hungry we were. Some of the girls were saying, 'Oh, you're really lucky, Racheal. You're so brown. Have you been on holiday?' and I said, 'No. I'm half-Sri Lankan.' To my horror, I heard someone mutter, 'So why are you doing Miss England?' I'd come such a long way from the days when people used to shout 'Paki' at me and bully me because of my race, but suddenly all those memories came flooding back and a wave of nausea washed over me as the thought struck me that maybe everyone was thinking I shouldn't be in the competition. I was mortified at my stupidity in never having realised it before, and felt I'd made a terrible mistake in believing I could take part.

A friend who's a journalist for a local newspaper told me later that she'd heard a reporter from a national newspaper say, 'I don't think Racheal Baughan's going to do very well. She looks really nervous and sad.' They were right, but what they didn't know was that it was the whispering behind my back that had put me in that state.

Although I knew I just had to try to carry on and forget about it, by the time I got back to my room I really felt I couldn't go through with it. So I phoned my brother James and said, 'I'm going to pull out. I don't want to do this. I just want to come home.'

I'm very close to James and, after I broke away a bit from Mum, he used to come to the television studios and sit with me for moral support. It was good to have him there, because Mum's so used to having to talk for me that she'd got out of the habit of letting me talk much for myself, whereas James is just quietly supportive.

James was adamant I shouldn't pull out, and said, 'Don't you dare let anyone make you feel like you don't belong there.' He reminded me that, despite all the bullying I'd experienced, I'd still managed to get this far. 'Don't let them do this to you, Racheal,' he insisted. 'They want you out of the competition. They're just trying to make you walk.'

'But I don't care,' I sobbed. 'I feel as though I've done what I needed to do. I just can't take being judged.' It felt as though I was already being judged, before I'd even gone in front of the judging panel, and the realisation began to dawn on me that perhaps, rather than jumping in at the deep end, I should have lowered myself slowly into the shallow end.

It's in my nature to try to do things I know I can't do. The BDD is always telling me I can't do things, which only makes me want to do them even more now. But it doesn't mean it's easy. Each time I reach the point of actually doing something, I think, 'What am I doing? I'm just putting myself in a stupid situation.'

As I sobbed down the telephone, James said, 'Racheal, we're so proud of you. We're so looking forward to seeing you up there. We really just want to have a happy ending to all this. Just remember why you're there.'

After talking to him, I realised I had to carry on, although once my confidence had been shaken there was really nothing anyone could do to make it any easier for me. But there were some absolutely lovely girls there – including some I'd heard rumoured weren't very nice – and they helped make up for the few bad ones.

That evening I felt worse than I'd done for years, but we had to go out for a celebratory dinner, so I spent the next few hours getting myself ready. It was really hard, because in my head I knew I could never live up to what I was up against, but I just had to keep reminding myself why I was there – not to be compared, but to face up to my fear.

After the dinner, I was with Amy Grove and Laura Shields – both really nice girls who are models now – and we went to look for a taxi to take us back to the hotel. There weren't many about, but Laura, who's very confident, just marched out into the road and hailed one as it passed, and we got in and shut the door. At that moment Danielle ran up and, not realising we were already in the taxi, opened the door and put her head inside. There was an empty seat beside me, so I smiled at her and said, 'You can get in if you want to.'

But she looked me up and down and said coldly, 'No, it's all right. I'll get the next one.'

I felt dreadful and when Amy and Laura suggested we go and have a drink in the hotel bar, I told them I just wanted to go to bed. 'Oh, come on. Don't be sensible,' they said. 'Come with us,' and, as I really liked them and didn't want to seem stand-offish, I agreed, and the three of us made our way to the bar for a nightcap.

As I was standing there, I was approached by a guy I'd never seen before, who, apparently out the blue, asked me, 'When you walked into the room with 36 of the most beautiful girls in the country, didn't you feel out of place?'

I was completely shocked. Why do people say such nasty

things? Even if they think them, why would they say them to someone they don't know anything about? Why would you want to hurt a total stranger? I don't know if Laura actually heard him, but she certainly must have seen my face drop, because she grabbed my arm and said, 'Is this guy bothering you? Come on. We're going to bed,' and she led me away. I was so grateful to her, because I don't know what I'd have done if she hadn't saved me. I felt absolutely devastated and spent the rest of the night in tears, feeling a pain that was almost physical.

It wasn't as though I'd just decided, 'Oh, I've had BDD, but I think I'll do Miss England. It'll be fine.' It wasn't fine. I desperately wanted to admit defeat and go home, but I knew my story had been an inspiration to other BDD sufferers and if I didn't go through with the competition I'd be letting them down and reinforcing their view that there was no hope for people with the illness – and I'd be letting down my family as well.

When I woke up the next morning, I felt as though I was going mad. James kept telling me, 'You've got to do it, Racheal. Believe me, it'll be fine,' and suddenly I just thought, 'You know what? I'm going to go with it. There are so many nice girls here and I've got this far. I'm not going to win, but so what? Does it really matter? I've been judged so much, and it's obvious that everyone will be looking at me and thinking, "What the hell is she doing here?" But it can't get much worse than it is already.'

The day of the final was quite boring, and we spent it rehearsing and getting ready. We were told to assemble for the 8am start of the rehearsal, and the few stragglers who came in at five minutes past eight got soundly told off. Then, an hour and a half later, Danielle turned up with curlers in her hair – and no one said a word. Perhaps it was because she's a professional beauty queen and has been in the business for so long that she knows everyone. But she was quite cocky and obviously didn't care anyway. I admire people who do that sort of thing, to a certain degree, and I couldn't help being impressed by her confidence, although I did feel it would be more impressive if she was also nicer to other people.

Before we went on stage, we had to go into a room and meet all the judges, and by that time I was really nervous. I took a deep breath outside the door and thought, 'Whether or not I'm here because Miss England wanted publicity for the competition, at least some people will be inspired. It's good for people with BDD to see someone doing something they never thought they could do, whatever it is. I'm going to see this through.' So I tried to walk into the room looking confident, although I was convinced the judges were all thinking, 'What's she doing here?'

Later, as I stood behind the curtain waiting to go out on the stage, I felt terrible. I don't know whether I was having a BDD attack, but I'd been convinced all day that my skin was really bad. The problem with BDD is that you actually create these things yourself. When I was really anxious, I'd pick at my skin until it was red and bleeding, so I made it bad even if it hadn't been bad before. I hadn't done that for years, but the night before the competition, when I couldn't sleep and was having an anxiety attack, I kept picking and pulling at my face, and had had to spend hours covering it up that morning.

I kept telling myself to see it as a presentation, like the ones I used to do for Esporta, and that the competition I was in was with BDD, not with any of the other girls.

When it came to my turn I made myself stand up tall, put my shoulders back and, mentally repeating my mantra 'Lights! Camera! Action!', I stepped out on to the stage with a smile on my face. I kept that smile in place the whole time and began to feel the first stirrings of pride in myself. It may sound a strange thing to say, as I wasn't even placed in the competition, but I did really well. I could see my mum, my brother and his wife and my boyfriend and friend in the audience, all with tears in their eyes, and I'd never seen them looking so proud. They, of all people, knew they were watching a girl who used to be too scared to walk through town.

After the competition I was absolutely ecstatic. My brother hugged me and said, 'You did so well! You were so professional I couldn't believe it. You really pulled it off. But you should have made the top 15!'

I just laughed and said, 'James, I don't mind. I feel I've won in my head. I've won a battle I've fought my whole life,' and I thought how proud Fay and Ethan would have been of me and how I'd somehow honoured their memories by doing the most difficult thing I could possibly have done.

To everyone else, it was just the Miss England competition, but to me it was so much more than that. It involved doing something massively different from anything I'd ever done in my life before, or ever thought I could do. It marked the end of my fear and the beginning of the rest of my life, and it was as though a huge weight had been lifted from me. I'd dared to do something that even a few weeks previously would have seemed unimaginable to me, and, much to my enormous surprise, the world hadn't come crashing down around me.

I looked a mess, my skin was terrible, but so what? It finally reinforced my growing belief that it *is* who I am on the inside that matters. I can't change what I look like, but that's only superficial anyway. What's important is that I *can* control what sort of person I am on the inside, and I can make my life what I want it to be by just taking chances and having the confidence to try.

I'd never felt as good as I did that day.

The confidence the competition gave me changed my life for a long time afterwards. I started going out with my friends at the weekends, partying and doing all the things I'd missed out on when I was younger, and I was determined to make the most of my life.

Before the competition I'd been cocooned within

environments in which I felt relatively safe. Working at Esporta, where everyone was so kind to me, and at Just GTIs, with my family around to protect me, I was still safely within my comfort zone. But all the coaching I'd had at the competition finally helped me to start being able to deal with the outside world as well. For example, the first time I went into town with my mum after the competition she said, 'I really notice a difference in you. I can't remember when I last saw you walking with your head up.'

One thing the experience of Miss England taught me was that a beautiful shell doesn't make you a beautiful person. No matter what you look like, how you behave can make you attractive – how you hold yourself, what you're like as a person, whether you allow your personality to shine through. I know many girls who may not be beautiful from a 'manufactured' point of view, but they shine as people and appear beautiful because of what's inside them.

I realised that if I try to show confidence – and smile – it makes a huge difference. And suddenly I was popular again. Before, I'd had to deal with the fear and misery that made me shrink inside a little more each time I went out into town and someone shouted abuse at me. But now people wanted to know me, and girls would approach me and chat to me.

Although some people asked me in tones of apparent wonder how I'd ever got into Miss England, I simply didn't care any more. I felt I'd been judged by Danielle when I first arrived at the competition, and I'd been judged by the man in the hotel bar, but now I just thought, 'Oh, leave me alone. So what?' Maybe I didn't deserve to be there, but I *was* there. I'd faced my fear and proved to myself that I was beating my battle against BDD, and no one was going to bring me down.

A little while ago I took part in a big charity auction in the County Mall in Crawley to raise money for Women's Aid, and there were teenagers coming up to me and hugging me, saying, 'You've been such an inspiration to us. Thank you for what you've done.' In reality it's my story that has been the inspiration for people, and I believe that the publicity it's received has helped stopped bullying in Crawley. There was a time when you'd go into the town centre and there'd be kids hanging around outside the shops hurling abuse at passers-by; some of them were really quite nasty. But now, because of all the local press coverage I've had, they smile at me and say hello. Wouldn't it be great if that could happen everywhere?

And that's why I felt angry about the way it seemed that Danielle behaved. She has an influence on young people – they look up to someone they see as 'cool' – and it's the responsibility of anyone in that position to use their influence to inspire people in a good way. Young people see Miss England as being something exciting, something they might like to do themselves, so they take notice of someone who's taken part in it. If I can say, 'Look at me. I've been bullied, but I've managed to do this,' that might make someone else who's been bullied think, 'Well, perhaps I'm not so bad.'

Because of what I learned through doing Miss England, I firmly believe in holding my head up no matter how bad I feel, and just by doing that I start to feel better. I used to do it at Esporta, because it felt like a safe place for me, but I needed to try to make everywhere a safe place. I don't care any more about being liked; what matters is feeling good, and the way I'm able to feel good is by deciding I'm going to be confident and happy with who I am. I'm not everybody's cup of tea, but no one can be, no matter who they are, and I think Miss England gave me the ability to feel like that.

I talk about doing Miss England as though I was better, but in reality I wasn't, although I was trying. It was the first competition I'd ever done, and I'd come a long way. When I went from working at Esporta to the completely unglamorous job at Just GTIs, it was as if I was trying to become the tomboy I was when I was young. But doing the competition brought my confidence out and was the real start of my recovery. It was a huge undertaking for anyone, let alone someone who has an enormous fear of being judged. But after what I'd faced and overcome, walking through town was going to be easy by comparison. It could have gone the other way, but thankfully it worked for me. Of course, I'm not saying to people, 'Oh, if you're ill just go and do something like that.' It wouldn't have worked if I'd tried to do it any sooner, but I was already 80 per cent recovered, and I think that was the right time for me.

In fact, I feel as though, as bad as some things have been, everything in my life has happened for a reason, and everything I've done in terms of the recovery from my illness has been done at just the right time. I had some huge setbacks at the beginning, but perhaps you have to have setbacks to enable you to move forward. You can't expect to face what is, in your particular circumstances, a massive goal and for everything to be OK. It's going to be difficult at first and you're going to be fearful. But if you keep pushing yourself just a little bit further over a period of time, which may be years, you'll get there eventually. The person I was pretending to be – a person who'd recovered from BDD – was eventually the person I became, because at least I was thinking positively and trying to get better.

Having said that, you can't fake your recovery: if you're not better, you're not going to be ready to deal with certain things. But at least you can try to do things and, each time you do, you get one step nearer to your goal.

Even now, it wouldn't be true to say that I'm 100 per cent; I'm never going to be 100 per cent with an illness like BDD. But I do believe you can learn to live with the illness and deal with it every day. You can get to the point where it never holds you back from anything you want to do – and I think that's quite an achievement.

21

Unwelcome Attention

Just before the Miss England competition, Trisha Goddard asked me to go on her show again, because she was so proud of how far I'd come since the last time she'd seen me. After the show I was invited to a party and I took Belinda with me.

As we were sitting at a table at the club, eating our barbecue, a pop singer (who I can't name for legal reasons) came over and started talking to us, although in fact he looks quite different in real life and I didn't recognise him.

After a while I asked if anyone knew where the toilet was, and the singer said, 'I'm going to the toilet. I'll show you.'

We walked across the room and he pointed out the Ladies. There was only one cubicle and, as I turned round to lock the door, it suddenly burst open and he was standing in front of me exposing himself! I laugh when I think about it now, but at the time I was really shocked and upset and simply couldn't believe it was happening. I was also very scared: there I was in the toilet with a celebrity standing in front of me with his trousers down, and with no cameras to prove that it wasn't a situation I'd either instigated or consented to. I felt the same helpless feeling I used to have when I was bullied, and I was thinking, 'What if he does something? No one would believe me.' Although my voice was quaking and I felt sick with fear, I managed to shout at him, 'What the hell are you doing? Get out!' And, much to my relief, he pulled up his trousers and left.

Apparently, when he went back to the table, someone asked him where I was and he replied curtly, 'I don't know,' and walked away.

When I came out of the toilet, I said to Belinda, 'I want to go. I'm really scared and I don't want to be around this situation.' It had a very disturbing effect on me – partly, I suppose, because of all the things I'd been through – and I was shaking with fear and anxiety.

Of course, it's completely wrong for anyone to flash at someone, no matter who they are. But what made it even more surprising was that the only words I'd exchanged with him had been, 'Hi,' 'Where do we get the barbecue from?', 'Are those peanut M&Ms?' and 'Where's the toilet?' We hadn't even engaged in a conversation because I'd been talking to someone else at our table.

Belinda is a journalist, and about a month later she told me she'd just spoken on the telephone to a journalist from a Sunday newspaper who'd said to her, 'I hear Racheal went back with [the singer] for a threesome at his place after the party,' and Belinda had replied, 'No, no. He just flashed at Racheal.'

'I'm really sorry,' Belinda told me, 'but a Sunday newspaper now knows about it.'

I couldn't believe it, and said, 'Surely as a journalist yourself you know they can now just make up whatever they like because you've validated it? If they print anything about it, I'm going to have to face going to court.'

I'd just wanted to keep the story quiet and forget about it, but if it was out in the open, I'd be forced to take some sort of action, if only to prove that what I said about it was true. I really didn't want that sort of publicity attached to my name, because what I'd been trying to do for so many years was show people how far I'd come, and that it is possible to recover from BDD. Imagine having all this singer's fans thinking I was a really bad person, because no one ever believes the girl in that type of situation, particularly when it's her word against that of someone with a good reputation, which he had at that time.

I'd told Paul about it when it happened and he'd wanted to go after the man, but I'd warned him to keep away, because I knew there was nothing he could do. But, despite the fact that Paul already knew about it, it would have been horrible for both of us if it had all been made public.

I was crying as I said to Belinda, 'I've just managed to build my confidence up and if the story is printed it'll kill me. You don't know what you've done.'

For the first time in a very long period I was ready to kill myself, because I'm so against that whole kiss-and-tell thing. I don't judge other people for doing it, but it's just not me, and I also knew that my brothers would want to kill the man involved. Although I knew I wasn't in any way to blame for it, the whole incident was something I was very embarrassed about and I certainly didn't want to share it with the rest of the world.

But the newspaper got in touch with me and said that if I didn't cooperate and tell them the whole story, they'd print their original story about the threesome. I was only 21, and very naive, so I was really upset. When I talked to my dad about it, he said, 'Racheal, they can't do that. You didn't do it and they can't lie. But if you tell them what actually did happen, they can print that. So it's best not to talk to them at all.'

But Belinda kept saying, 'No, Racheal. If you don't talk to them, they *will* do that story.'

In the end I agreed to the journalist coming down to see to me, and told him, 'I'm not going to talk to you about this and, if you're going to write about it, I don't want my name to be used. I don't want people to think I've told you about it. I need a contract signed by the newspaper confirming that you're never going to say I said anything about it.'

So he brought a contract with him but inevitably it was a lot more in their favour than in mine and I wouldn't sign it.

The newspaper was offering £10,000 for the story, to be split between Belinda and me. She kept trying to persuade me to tell the story, saying, 'Oh, come on, Racheal. We'll have a holiday.' But I refused – £5,000 (or any amount of money) in exchange for having a reputation as a slanderer, however undeserved, didn't seem a very good deal. It wasn't just that my reputation with the public was at stake, but my family would have been completely crushed. I know what happened wasn't my fault, but the story they were going to write was really bad, and I felt everyone would think I was just another of those girls who tell awful stories to the papers. I just didn't want that kind of publicity. It was hard enough making myself talk to the media about my illness, let alone something like that.

When the journalist came to see me, he wanted me to phone the singer while he recorded our conversation, but of course I refused. I was determined I wasn't going to validate the story in any way. Belinda was there at the time and she suddenly said, 'I'll do it.' She couldn't get hold of him, so instead she spoke to a friend of his, another singer who'd been there that night, and said to him, 'The papers know about him flashing at Racheal.' His friend didn't deny it, but just angrily referred to 'you bloody nobodies' and put the phone down. I couldn't believe what was happening: there I was in tears while the reporter taped Belinda's phone conversation.

The only reason I'd agreed to the reporter coming to see me at all was because I wanted to sign something that confirmed that whatever they said hadn't come from me, and in the end they couldn't use the story because I refused to cooperate and validate it. But both Belinda and the reporter were putting a lot of pressure on me, and I can see how people get sucked in to doing something like that – and then live to regret it.

This singer was a big name at the time, and I knew that, if I said anything, everything else I was trying to do would be forgotten and I'd be remembered only as the girl who he flashed at – or worse.

Funnily enough, recently – five years later – he tried to contact me through MySpace, sending me messages saying he'd like to meet up. I thought at first it was a fake profile or that he was having a laugh, because I couldn't believe that, after what he'd done to me, he had the audacity to try to contact me. Perhaps he didn't remember me, but I knew it was him, because he had also been contacting model friends of mine via the same website, and I simply ignored it.

What was particularly bad about that incident was that, if the story had been printed, I would have felt that everyone thought I was full of crap, and I don't think I could have lived with that. I can laugh about it now, but at the time it was very stressful and very embarrassing, and all I wanted to do was hide. I've always been very 'prudey', so that sort of thing is particularly distressing for me. I knew Paul wasn't going to turn against me because of it, because he knew it wasn't my fault, but if it had been made public, it would really have knocked me back, and I certainly wouldn't have done the Miss England competition.

To make it all even worse, I discovered the newspaper had taken sneaky pictures of me leaving my house, which made me feel absolutely awful, as though I'd been violated. Although I was much better by this time, I still hated the thought of being seen when I didn't want to be seen. I was working at Just GTIs and not wearing any make-up, which was fine in front of my brother and the people at work, but I didn't want other people to see me like that. I was terrified that the pictures they'd taken would show me looking terrible, and that in itself would have been bad enough, even without any story.

But, apart from all that, it was a really sad experience for me, because it seemed to show that you can't really trust anyone outside your own family.

22

The Samaritans

When I was really ill, my mum gave me the phone number of the Samaritans (see p.271) and I'd phone them as a kind of release when I was having an attack and felt like self-harming. Being able to talk to someone who didn't know who I was and who didn't try to reassure me or give me advice was a tremendous help to me at the time. So I was really pleased when I was offered the opportunity to give something back to them after all they'd done for me.

Just after the Miss England competition, someone from the Guildford branch of the Samaritans sent me an email and asked if I'd take part in some talks with them. I think they'd seen me on some of the TV programmes I'd done and thought I might be able to help them deal with people with BDD and similar illnesses who phone them up. They were particularly interested in talking to me because I'd mentioned in an interview that I used to phone them when I was ill, and they don't often get the chance to find out what happens to people who've called them.

They'd been absolutely fantastic to me and had literally saved my life on more than one occasion, so I was happy to agree to go to one of their conferences in Guildford and talk about my experiences.

I sat in a chair in front of an audience of about 500 of their volunteers while they asked me questions, and I was really nervous to begin with. But, in a strange way, talking about the illness somehow helps me to detach myself from it. It's like talking about *something*, a separate entity, rather than about *me*, which makes it easier. So, although I was very anxious to begin with, I felt a lot calmer once I started talking. I'd learned by that time to shut the world out when I needed to, and the fact that people were looking at me for a reason, because they were listening to what I was saying, made me less uncomfortable.

The key thing for people with BDD is that they aren't really looking for reassurance; they just want to talk to someone and get it all off their chest, and being able to do so might just stop them self-harming – or worse. Talking to someone over the phone who isn't judging you or telling you that your fears are unfounded is a way of releasing the pain you feel inside. So I wanted to make the point at the conference that the volunteers mustn't ever feel they haven't helped: just being on the end of the phone and listening is enough.

It was very touching and very rewarding, because everyone there was so kind to me. At the end of the talk, an elderly man came over, gave me a hug and said that it was the saddest story he'd ever heard and that I'd been an inspiration.

After that, I started getting emails from various regional areas, and then two of the Samaritans' main directors came to meet me at my house. As a result of that meeting, I was asked to do conferences up and down the country, in all sorts of places, including prisons, and to talk about dealing with a whole range of illnesses associated with eating disorders, self-harm and depression. So I'm going to be working quite closely with the Samaritans in the future, which I'm really looking forward to, because they're all amazing people.

Although I can talk for England – I just keep going and going until someone stops me – I've recently begun to get a bit tearful when I discuss what happened in the past, which is odd because I never used to be like that. But I think perhaps it's because I now feel I've left it all behind, and it's almost as though I'm talking about another little girl, a sad little girl who I feel really sorry for.

Because of my connection with the Samaritans, I was also recently asked to participate in a 'celebrity auction' they were organising on eBay, alongside celebrities such as *Shipwrecked* stars Lianne Dauban, Louis Rennocks, Naomi Millbank-Smith and Sophie Wardman, as well as the Channel 4 reality-TV show's overall winner, Ben Lunt, and the founder of *Big Issue*, John Bird. The auction was run to raise funds for the Samaritans and help create more awareness of the charity, and taking part was the least I could do after all the support they've given me over the years. But, even so, I was dreading the embarrassment of receiving no bids at all, although, to my surprise – and enormous relief – I ended up raising a respectable amount.

23

True Model Media

After the Miss England competition, I received offers for modelling, but it wasn't something I wanted to pursue. I've always been interested in make-up and designing my own clothes, and in the industry as a whole, but not in the actual modelling, not least because I like to be able to approve my pictures – and modify them using Photoshop when necessary – which I obviously wouldn't be able to do.

In fact, one of my ambitions is to learn more about photography. Perhaps it's something to do with the illness, but I don't really want other people to take pictures of me, and I've taken a lot of the ones people see of me, or they've been taken by photographers I know and trust. Something that is definitely due to the illness is that I need to have Mum's approval before I let anyone else see them, because I don't like any of them – except the ones that don't look like me – although I realise now that what I'm seeing isn't necessarily what other people are seeing. I Photoshop them and show them to Mum to find out what she thinks, and she says, 'Racheal, what *have* you done to your face? You've changed it!'

Then we'll argue about which one is better and eventually she'll say, 'Racheal, just listen to your mother,' and I'll end up having to use one that's not edited. Mum acts like my mirror and I trust her and know she'll always tell me if a photo isn't good – and, equally, if it is – and I know I'm lucky to have her.

I realise that, because of my illness, I have unrealistic expectations of what I want to look like. Given the chance, I'd try to change everything about my appearance with Photoshop, but what's interesting is that, when I do change something, Mum always thinks I've ruined my face. It just proves that surgery is never the right thing for BDD sufferers, as we already see something completely different from what the rest of the world sees. I heard somewhere that Michael Jackson suffers from BDD, and of course he's got the money to be able to make his face everything he wants it to be, but I'm sure everyone would agree that he looked much better before.

So, although it's very nice to be offered all sorts of work, it isn't realistic to think I'd be able to accept it if someone took photographs of me and said, 'That's great. We'll decide which ones we want to use.'

But it seemed such a waste to have made all those contacts and not be able to put them to good use, and then one day the idea just popped into my head to start a model agency. I'd met a lot of pretty girls at the Miss England competition and I knew there were a lot of talented girls that I could put forward for the work I was being offered, and that they'd be really glad to have it. So I started True Model Media, and it's worked really well. I've always felt uncomfortable about turning down offers, because it seems so rude, but now, when I'm asked to do something, I say, 'I can't do it because I'm unavailable, but I do have a girl on my books who could.'

Another reason why I've been teaching myself photography is because I want to be able to put together portfolios for the girls who work for my model agency. I think a lot of women feel more comfortable posing for another woman, particularly when they're doing bikini shots and that sort of thing.

I started off using my web-design experience to do websites for about ten girls I'd become friendly with at Miss England, and that gradually led to their doing fashion shows for local boutiques and small designers. It was work I really enjoyed, and I realised it was something I could focus on, and it's just grown from there. Owing to client demand, I've also recently started to take on male models, and now have around 500 models on the books and the work is coming in steadily. So I'm really busy with the agency and often work until three in the morning, putting together the models' web profiles and promoting them. But what's most important is that True Model Media already has a good name.

I'm also working in association with the Miss England organisers, and part of the prize for the girls in the competition in 2007 was for all the finalists and the top three girls in each regional heat to be signed up by True Model Media.

I still receive offers of work from people who've seen articles about me in the newspapers, or who saw me in Miss England. For example, recently I was asked to model jewellery at a very exclusive hotel in Dubai. Although it's a beautiful place, I just didn't want to do it, but I was able to pass the contact on to my own agency's models. That way it doesn't seem as though I'm missing opportunities, because I sort of have them by proxy.

However, I do sometimes feel as though I'm letting Fay and Ethan down by turning down offers. At one point, I became almost obsessed about forcing myself to accept them – modelling and otherwise – because I felt that being offered opportunities was like a blessing: you're very lucky if people headhunt you. But I realise now that it's not just BDD that makes me turn them down. I'm not a model – in the sense that I don't have that passion that you need to do modelling – and they're things that simply aren't me; they're obviously not what I want to do, otherwise I'd do them.

When I was growing up and had an eating disorder, the average size for a model was UK size 8 or 10, which is a healthy size, particularly for someone who's five feet ten – just think of all those beautiful, curvy top models like Claudia Schiffer and Cindy Crawford. But now it's size 4, which is an American size 0. So I also thought that running my own model agency might give me a chance to exert a small amount of influence in the industry. Not only would it enable me to have a career after all I'd missed out on, but, more importantly, it would also give me the opportunity to try to provide better role models for young girls.

With that in mind, I recently set up the S.O.S. (Stop 0 Size) campaign and only take on models of a healthy size, whatever that is for the individual girl. I've been asked why I take on surgically enhanced models if I'm promoting healthy role models for young girls, but I see that as something rather different, and I can't control everything. I see no reason to discriminate against a girl who's already had surgery because, most importantly, it's not health damaging in the way that extreme dieting is, and it's the health factor I'm focusing on. While I'd never encourage any girl to have surgery to further her career, I won't judge her for it.

Modelling is usually a very cutthroat and cold industry, and the girls – a lot of whom are already very insecure – are often treated like commodities or products. But the most important thing to me, even above the clients, is the girls themselves, and I'm proud that they feel able to approach me and talk to me about their problems, which they may find easier to do because they know I've had problems myself.

If my insistence that the girls who work for True Model Media are a healthy size means I'm unable to find them work in certain fields – such as high fashion at the moment – then I'd rather not get them work in those fields anyway. I'm not prepared to pass on a client's message to a particular girl that she needs to lose inches off her hips, or whatever else their requirements might be. But that's OK, because there's plenty of other work available for them that doesn't require them to starve themselves until they're unhealthily skinny.

When I'm promoting the agency, some designers say to me, 'I'm sorry, but the clothes look better on a girl who's skinny.' Well, I'd actually regard a girl of size 8 or 10 as skinny, although I think that in itself is avoiding the main issue, which is that designers should cater for women of all sizes. If you're a good designer or a good tailor, you should be making clothes for the *real* women who want to buy them. It's easy to tailor for size 0 – you might as well send a coat hanger down the catwalk. The average woman in the UK is size 14, so, if designers can't make clothes that look good on a size 8, perhaps they should be re-examining their own skills rather than putting the onus on the models. Designs that are made for size 0 simply aren't going to look good on someone bigger; the tailoring is going to be completely wrong. I'm a size 8 and I struggle to find clothes for myself, and so do many of my friends and the models at the agency, so what hope is there for 'normal-sized' women?

But that doesn't mean I have a specific size limit, or any height restriction, because, for example, a lingerie model who's five feet one and a size 6 can be perfectly healthy. Nor do I discriminate against girls who are naturally slim, but it's fairly obvious when someone's 'unnaturally' skinny and is going too far with dieting. If I thought a girl was struggling to be a size 8 and that it wasn't her natural size, I'd encourage her to reach whatever is a healthy size for her. I really don't think that size is a factor in whether or not someone's attractive or whether or not she's able to model. It's a hard industry and models need to be able to take the pressure and remain healthy.

Whenever I'm doing shoots, and when I was doing a

documentary recently, I make sure there's loads of food in the studio, which is the opposite of what happens at other places: I've been on castings where there's no food to be found anywhere. Apparently, True Model Media has a reputation among the models for its lovely food. I employ caterers and we put out all different kinds of foods, including salads and cakes, and what's funny is that the cakes and all the fatty foods are the first things to be eaten.

I really do feel that it's sad – and ridiculous – that the industry is so size orientated. Miss England 2006 is a beautiful girl called Eleanor Glynn, but apparently her agency told her she was too big and needed to lose weight – which, at size 8 and five feet nine, is absurd. But people are very cold about telling girls to come back when they've lost some weight. So I was very glad to hear that she wasn't prepared to do it.

Although it makes me unpopular in some quarters, I refuse to bow down to the demands of the business if it means that the girls are being encouraged to be unhealthy, and that young girls who see them as role models are encouraged to diet as well. I'd rather stick with commercial work, which, although it doesn't make as much money as high fashion, enables the girls to remain fit and well.

In fact, most of the smaller designers are quite happy to use normal-sized girls; it's just the bigger names that insist on their models being really thin. They say to me, 'The thing is, Racheal, if a model's getting paid to do a job, she's getting paid to look a certain way.' I try to point out the ripple effect that has on everybody else, on all the people who aren't getting paid to be unhealthily thin. For example, no one's paying my niece, who's a size 8 and getting the mickey taken out of her at school because she's not size 0, and who came to me recently and said, 'Am I too fat, Auntie Racheal?' That's tragic, and it's wrong.

I'm very excited at the moment because we're about to move

to new premises, complete with a brand-new studio. It's still in the process of being decorated and refurbished, but is already looking fantastic. I've been to various agencies in the past – after Miss England, when people wanted to sign me up – and, although they might be in the middle of quite a good area, some of them are just little offices above shops. But my place will be really impressive, and somewhere people will enjoy coming to. My brother James is going to open a beauty salon next door, and there's a costume shop next door to that, so everything will be available in one place.

Having the studio will enable me to offer complete packages for small designers, for people who want their clothes modelled but don't really know how to go about it, as well as for beauty shoots, jewellery shops and so on. People will be able to come to one place and have everything done for them. We'll provide the models, the studio and the photographs and, making use of my own graphic-design skills, will also make their files, get their billboards sorted out and even help with their websites.

I like the idea of catering for smaller businesses, which no one else seems to do at the moment. I doubt whether someone who has a little boutique selling beautiful items would think of contacting Models 1, for example; they just wouldn't know where to start. So a package deal covering the cost of the studio, the models and everything else at an affordable price, with everything done in one place, will be really useful for them. It will also mean that the models' profiles won't have to be all web based, because I'll be able to keep a catalogue for people to look through when they come in.

So, although it involves a huge amount of work and many late nights, I'm really enjoying it all, not least because none of it would have seemed even remotely possible just a few short years ago.

24

Miss Great Britain 2006

One day in 2006, I received a generic email giving details of the latest Miss Great Britain competition. It explained that regional heats were going to be held up and down the country, the closest to me being London, and it all sounded very exciting and glamorous and the perfect opportunity for me to scout for models for True Model Media. Taking part in Miss England had increased my confidence enormously and I knew that this time I'd have nothing to lose by attending the event. I wouldn't need to be afraid of being judged, because I wouldn't be entering the competition in the hope of winning, but rather because it would give me the chance to do some networking for the agency.

So I sent in a couple of photos and, to my delight, was invited to attend the London heat. However, as I read the part in the second email about a swimwear round, I realised I couldn't do it. There had only been evening-wear and club-wear rounds in Miss England, and just the thought of having to wear a bikini made me feel light-headed with anxiety.

I'd recently started to have what I call a 'lapse' after a friend had asked me to go swimming with her one day. The old fear returned at the thought of wearing a swimsuit in public and I ended up letting her down. I was really disappointed when I realised that yet again I was allowing BDD to hold me back from facing what was, after all, a relatively small challenge. But it felt as though it would be giving people the opportunity to judge me, which was something I simply couldn't bring myself to face. Wearing swimwear for photographs was one thing, as some judicious airbrushing with Photoshop made me look quite acceptable, but the prospect of wearing it in 'real life' seemed very different and I was sure people would be disgusted by my revolting body.

The night before I was due to go swimming with my friend I tried on every type of swimwear I could lay my hands on in the hope of finding something that would cover me up adequately. But nothing seemed to work, and for the first time in ages the frustration and anxiety led me to have a BDD attack. I was very disappointed in myself for allowing BDD to win, and was terrified at the thought that I might be going backwards, because that would mean I'd not only let down my friend and myself, but I'd also let down all the people who'd believed in me and who'd taken inspiration from what I'd done and perhaps felt that their own lives could be turned around too.

So, although my immediate reaction on reading the email from Miss Great Britain was that I couldn't go through with the competition after all, having thought about it long and hard, I decided it was something I had to do. Looking back, it almost seems as though it was fate giving me the opportunity to face my ultimate fear, and it came just at the right time to stop me slipping backwards and giving in to the ever-present threat of BDD. I knew that many of the top magazines would be covering the Miss London competition and that, if my model agency was going to be successful, I simply couldn't turn down any opportunities to further my business. After all, there was nothing to say I couldn't wear a sarong with my bikini to stop me feeling quite so exposed.

When I arrived for Miss London, the atmosphere seemed rather cold and I had to fight my rising nervousness and try to ignore the small voice in my head suggesting that this might be a good time to turn and run. Fortunately, I was saved by being greeted by a warm and beautiful girl called Ashley, who is one of the Miss Great Britain organisers and who instantly made me feel at ease, and I was soon making friends and enjoying the rehearsals.

Then, before I knew it, the competition was about to start, and the nerves returned with a vengeance. However, a couple of glasses of champagne helped to calm me down a bit, and I kept saying over and over in my head, 'Come on, Racheal. You can do this,' and reminding myself that, if I allow my personality to shine through, people concentrate less on judging me on what I look like.

Walking out wearing my bikini in front of all those people was one of the hardest things I'd ever done. I'd completely covered my body in fake tan and oils in the hope that they'd act as a disguise, and I knew that all I could do was try to keep smiling. Needless to say, I wasn't placed in the competition, and the title was won by a lovely girl called Kelly Richards, who's now a friend of mine as well as one of my models.

I went home that day feeling satisfied and full of adrenalin. I'd spoken with lots of people, made some good contacts for the agency and signed up some wonderful girls. But most of all I'd faced the BDD and shown it once again that it could no longer control me. I feel as though I'm locked in a constant battle with the illness, but I will never allow it to win. My family were very proud of me, and knowing I'd proved how much better I was gave me an overwhelming sense of achievement that made it all worthwhile.

A few days later I received an email from the Miss Great Britain organisers asking if I wanted to attend another heat, but I wrote back saying that, although I'd had a wonderful time, I didn't feel up to doing it all again so soon afterwards. They responded by asking if they could put my photograph in the photo heat and, figuring I had nothing to lose, I agreed.

Three weeks after that, I was shocked to receive an email saying something along the lines of: 'Congratulations! You have won the photo heat and we would like to invite you to compete in the Miss Great Britain 2006 finals.'

I had to read it again to double-check that it was real, and was immediately terrified. As much as it was an honour to be invited to take part, I knew I wasn't good enough. But then I remembered the promise I'd made myself about not allowing BDD to make me turn down opportunities, however daunting, and I reminded myself how much stronger I was. It was going to be a very grand event, with three nights in a top five-star hotel in London, rubbing shoulders with some of the best and most influential people in the industry. I could wear a sarong again, which had helped me to feel less exposed in the Miss London competition – and, after all, what was the worst that could happen? So I accepted and began to feel quite excited about it all.

As photographs of all the other finalists started appearing on the website, I looked through them for potential models for my agency, and there were some great girls. Then one day there was a photo of Danielle Lloyd right next to the one of me. My heart sank and I knew I couldn't go through with it. Part of me knew it was ridiculous to allow myself to be reduced to a state of anxiety, but the memory of how I'd felt at the Miss England competition a couple of years previously came flooding back, and I really didn't think I could go through that again. So I told my mum I was going to pull out.

But I think Mum felt there might always be something that could potentially stand in the way of my taking advantage of the opportunities I was being offered. She reminded me that I hadn't agreed to enter the competition because I wanted or expected to win it, but because it was going to be a great chance to network and make contacts that would help the girls already on the books of True Model Media. She was right, of course, and there was nothing for it but to take myself in hand and go through with it. If I wasn't going to let BDD beat me, I certainly couldn't let myself be beaten by anyone's subtly undermining remarks.

When I arrived at the London hotel, I felt extremely nervous, but grateful for the opportunity the organisers had given me by allowing me to attend and compete in the final. I knew I was never going to be on the same level as the other competitors, but that meant I didn't have to try to compete and could just enjoy myself.

As I walked though the glass doors, I was greeted by the smiling face of Kelly, the Miss London winner, and instantly felt more relaxed and able to start mingling with the other girls, who, much to my enormous relief, were all really nice. Then suddenly the atmosphere changed and everything went quiet, and I turned round to see Danielle entering the hotel looking confident and self-assured. Trying to ignore the sickening pain in my stomach, I told myself firmly not to be so silly.

There's a certain amount of paranoia associated with BDD in that you feel as though people are talking about you behind your back, and I told myself I had probably imagined Danielle's previous hostility towards me. So, to prove it to myself, and for the sake of being polite, I decided to go over to her to say, 'Hello.' But, as she returned my greeting with a casual 'Hi', I felt that she gave me that same up-and-down appraising look that again sent shivers down my spine and made me wonder what she could see that was so wrong with me. My confidence immediately dropped and the same anxiety and insecurity I'd felt when our paths last crossed came flooding back.

But this time I felt that Danielle's attitude towards me changed throughout the competition, leaving me very confused and uncomfortable. Perhaps I was misunderstanding things but one minute, whenever anyone important was in sight, she'd put her arm around me and be my best friend, and then, as soon as the person had gone, she'd return to ignoring me. I kept telling myself that it was my imagination, or that perhaps she simply didn't like me, and it was that knowledge that was undermining my already shaky confidence. But, whatever the reason, of all the girls in the competition, she was the only one who was able to make me feel so completely out of my depth that I wanted to go home.

When the night of the pre-competition party came, I fought the desire to hide myself away in my room and did my best to put a smile on my face and attend the party. It must have been one of our 'friends' occasions, as, while I was talking to some people, Danielle came over to join us and stood next to me. They asked her who she was and she replied, 'I was Miss England 2004 and tomorrow I will be taking home the Miss Great Britain title too.' Her confidence was impressive.

As the final of the competition came closer, I was overwhelmed with nerves. We'd been rehearsing from 7am until 10pm every day and, although I was having fun, I'd started to look very run down and tired. So I decided to change my appearance in some way, because I felt that wearing a 'disguise' would help me to remember it was a show and to feel more confident in front of the judges and the star-studded audience. Unfortunately, the appearance change I chose was to curl my hair, which proved to be a very bad decision. As I looked in the mirror, all I could see was the girl from the past, and I felt physically sick as memories of the time when I was so ill flooded back. Also, my anxious state of mind wasn't helped by the fact that I'd picked up an ear infection that was affecting my hearing and balance. Things were getting progressively worse.

At the Miss London competition, I'd really enjoyed helping the other girls get ready, showing them how to cover marks and acting out the career as a make-up artist I'd missed out on. So this time, as I was finishing putting on my make-up, using the one mirror that had to be shared among 50 of us, I was surrounded by girls wanting to borrow things and asking me to help them with their hair and so on. Suddenly I realised I'd spent so much time helping everyone else that I didn't have any time left for myself, and I rushed to apply my make-up in a state of panic. Inevitably, the result was a complete mess, and it was only the thought that my family had paid £200 each for their tickets to the final that stopped me pulling out of the competition.

Then, to make things worse, just before it came to walking out on to the stage, I realised that the dress I was wearing, courtesy of a generous sponsor, was too large at the top and kept falling down. Horrified, I quickly ran back to the changing room to grab some of my sticky tape, only to find that someone had taken it. But time had run out and there was nothing for it but to run back and get in line to enter the stage, with my hair looking as though I'd just slept on it and holding up my dress with one hand.

I cringe even now when I think about the disaster I looked that night, but even so my overwhelming feeling is one of pride that, despite all the knock-backs, I managed to go through with it and to make myself just a little bit stronger than I'd been before.

I sent Danielle an email afterwards to say 'Congratulations!' The rumours that had been flying around must have been hurtful, and I believe in giving people the benefit of the doubt, not least because I know myself how upsetting it is to be aware of negative things being said behind your back. But I never received a reply, and the next thing I knew, stories about the relationship she'd allegedly had with Teddy Sheringham *before* the competition were all over the papers, and not long afterwards she was stripped of her title although later the allegation was withdrawn.

25

A Hidden Agenda

One day in February 2007, I had a phone call from someone who said he was a journalist for a newspaper and wanted to work with me to make one of my models the next Kelly Brook. Although it was a bit naive of me to take what he said at face value, it seemed such a fantastic opportunity for one of my models that I was really excited – for a few seconds.

'What we'll do,' he said, 'is set up one of your models in various situations with celebrities so that she ends up going home with them.'

So it *was* too good to be true! What he seemed to be suggesting was that I use one of the girls as bait so he could write stories about celebrities.

'That's not the kind of thing we do,' I told him.

He was obviously irritated, and snapped back, 'Well, that's how all the other agencies work. They all do that,' and he mentioned some of the big commercial agencies who concentrate on glamour work rather than high fashion.

His attitude suddenly changed completely and he started

making accusations about the girls working as escorts. I was really shocked and very upset at the way he was talking to me, trying to undermine me and suggest that I didn't know anything about the model business. But perhaps what struck me most during the conversation was the fact that he kept contradicting himself, either unknowingly or with scant regard for what he was actually saying. Having asked me to consent to using one of the girls to set traps for celebrities, which he agreed was escorting and which he said is what other agencies do, he then accused me of running an escort agency. When I'm talking to someone, I listen very carefully to what they're saying and I kept thinking, 'That's not what you told me previously,' and gradually the truth started to come out – although I expect someone like that has forgotten what the truth is.

He seemed to think I should be honoured that he was suggesting working with me, and the very professional-sounding way he talked was obviously an attempt to make me feel insecure and uncomfortable. But he was also slipping into the conversation all sorts of questions such as what I thought about the organisation of Miss England and Miss Great Britain, and he said some pretty salacious things about the organisers, which I told him were definitely untrue.

He was both extremely critical of my business and intent on telling me how to run it. For example, he said I had to be registered with the Association of Models, which I'd already looked into and in fact isn't the case, because they're more of a promotional and marketing set-up, as I'd learned when I'd registered with the Department of Trade and Industry. So it became obvious that he didn't really know what he was talking about – at least in some respects – and I realised it was just a tactic: if you make someone feel small, it might make them talk and then they might give an unguarded opinion that you can twist around and use as a quote – 'Racheal Baughan said...' He also kept going on about Danielle Lloyd, how lovely she is and what a beautiful girl she is. Again, I think he was hoping I'd say something quotable, but I just kept repeating, 'Mmm, mmm.'

However, for whatever reason, he did give me some good advice about how important it is to raise the profiles of my models and to be fussy about who I take on because of how it reflects on the image of the agency – not rocket science for anyone involved in any type of business.

Then he suddenly said, 'I need a client list from you,' and when I told him my client list is confidential, he replied, 'Well, I could phone up Models 1 or Select and they'd give me their client lists.'

'I think you'd find they wouldn't,' I said. 'They can't disclose that kind of information.'

It became apparent pretty quickly that he was expecting me to be stupid – some kind of brainless bimbo – and he became very abusive when he didn't get the information he seemed to want. People like that work by waiting until you say something in a slightly wrong way and then they twist it, and he obviously thought he'd extracted some sort of useful information from me because he asked me to meet him in person at the newspaper's offices. The only other reason I could think of for his request, in view of my mostly guarded or ambiguous answers to his questions, was that he wanted to be able to film me going into the offices so he could say, 'This is what Racheal Baughan said when she came into the office to talk to me.' But, whatever his reasons, I felt I'd already heard enough from him to be convinced that the last thing on his mind was helping me or any of my models.

Some of the facts he was telling me, including how one of the winners of Miss Great Britain has been involved as a high-class escort, seemed very dubious and unlikely from my own experience and knowledge of the people concerned and I found his attitude towards me very bullying and upsetting. It was disappointing after having initially thought he was offering an opportunity for one of my girls to get regular work through a contract with his newspaper. But I did think that what he was suggesting all sounded a bit dodgy, and I'd very quickly become suspicious of his true motives, not least because it's normally someone from a newspaper's picture desk who contacts me to book models, not a journalist.

After the phone call, I spoke to my mum and told her I thought it was all rather fishy, and – being the sort of mother she is, and not caring what people think about her when it comes to protecting me – she phoned him.

At first he wouldn't speak to her when she said she was from True Model Media, so she had to tell him she was my mother and that she was phoning to say we needed to have a statement in writing to confirm that the newspaper wasn't going to use me for any kind of story. Unfortunately, while trying to make him understand how hard I worked, she told him I'd got myself into debt setting up the agency and also that I'd just signed a contract with a yacht company to send some of the girls out to Monaco later in the year. I know she only wants to protect me and that she was trying to make me sound good, but it would have been better if she hadn't said anything to him at all, because he was only going to interpret it in whatever way best suited his own purposes.

He phoned me again later and was really annoyed and said, in a very hectoring manner, 'I don't appreciate your mother phoning me. It's entirely unprofessional. I don't need some battleaxe phoning me up and giving me a whole load of waffle. So, you're in debt. Have you got the girls in debt? And I understand your girls *are* doing escort work.'

The thought that someone might think I'd got the girls in debt was very distressing, particularly as I work so hard and they're what matters to me more than anything. And I was completely shocked at his suggestion that True Model Media was a front for an escort agency, and simply couldn't understand what he meant.

'Is it any of your business what your work colleagues get up to after they work for your newspaper?' I asked him.

'Well, no,' he replied.

'Well,' I said, 'I have 400 models on my books, and what they might or might not do outside True Model Media is out of my control. What I care about is getting them the modelling and promotional work I deal with.'

'Well, you're sending them out to Monaco to be on yachts with men,' he said.

'Excuse me? Are you saying that you regard leaflet distribution as escorting?' I asked him coldly.

'Well,' he replied, 'it could be seen as escorting.'

I was furious. 'No, it could not be seen as escorting,' I told him. 'It involves handing out leaflets and key rings.'

'Well, I don't regard that as modelling,' he said nastily.

'It's promotions,' I answered. 'It's what I deal with. If you look at the website, it says TV extras, modelling and *promotions*. That's what I do. As I explained to you before, because of my S.O.S. campaign, I can't go against what I believe in and work with the bigger designers.'

To my amazement, he stared shouting at me, in a very unprofessional way. 'How do I know you're not just using the girls to run an escort agency? How can we work with any of your girls?'

'Look,' I said, 'if you don't want to work with the agency, that's fine. But if you do, I need it in writing that you're meeting me on a business and professional basis to book models and that you're not going to use anything *I* say in an article.'

'Huh,' he answered sneeringly. 'The first you'd know about it would be when it came out in the newspaper.'

Reeling somewhat from his unpleasant tone, but anxious not to antagonise him too much, I agreed to a meeting – to which I actually had no intention of going – and he said he'd send me a contract that afternoon. Not surprisingly, the contract never arrived and, to be honest, even if he'd been a genuine client, I'd have turned down the business, because there aren't any circumstances under which I'm prepared to work with someone who's rude to me and who sneers at my girls or my agency.

After my conversation with this journalist, I rang Ashley, one of the organisers of Miss Great Britain. Mum had already phoned her to tell her that a reporter was asking loads of questions, because she was worried that, if I'd said anything that could be misinterpreted, he might twist it round into something that sounded really bad. I hadn't said anything – because there was nothing bad to say – but we still thought we'd better tell Ashley that the newspaper was fishing around for information. As it turned out, he'd apparently already been in touch with them, pretending to be from some kind of business that wanted to sponsor Miss Great Britain for £250,000. It was then that I realised it probably wasn't just my agency he was after.

After Miss Great Britain 2006 I had been asked to take part in Miss Hawaiian Tropic. Although I'd turned it down, there was apparently a journalist there who wanted to talk to me, which seemed strange because I had only 12 girls on my books at the time. Was it the same man? I wonder. If so, he's been investigating me since 2006. But what for? I can't see how I might have been worth investigating then, unless he was hoping I was someone who'd be prepared to do anything to raise the profile of my new agency, and that I might be a potential source of salacious stories about other people he was really after. Or perhaps he was hoping to use my connection with the Miss Great Britain organisation to get at them.

Although I was very upset by the journalist's bullying manner, by the end of our conversation I couldn't help laughing and said, 'You can keep on digging but you're never going to find anything. There's nothing to find out about me that people don't already know.'

He eventually told me that the source of his 'information' about my girls working as escorts was a girl who'd taken part in Miss Hawaiian Tropic. But I don't believe him. I do so much for the girls and I'd be very upset if I thought one of them might say something about me to a sleazy person like that. A lot of them are my friends and they're people I really care about, but some of the girls are only 17 and I do worry that it might be very tempting for them to lie about me if they were offered money and a chance to break into the industry.

So, although I don't have any worries about what he can truthfully say about me, he really disturbed me at the time and it was a big setback, because I suddenly felt I couldn't be bothered any more. I was finally starting to build a career for myself which, at one time when I was so ill, I didn't think was ever going to be possible. Everything had been going so well and I was so excited about it all, and then I get someone like that shouting at me on the phone and calling my mum a battleaxe. But people like that don't care; they're quite happy to tread on other people's feelings and even to make them ill if it gets them a good story. It was obvious he was just using bullying tactics to try to get whatever it was he wanted, and that his offer to help one of the girls was bogus, and I did feel proud of myself for standing up against him. But it was hard, and the last thing I needed when I'm working day and night to do something positive and something that will give me a future.

Perhaps, being such an apparently nasty person himself, he couldn't understand that there are some people who'll actually work for nothing, in my case because I care about the girls and because finding jobs for them gives me satisfaction. But he's gone very quiet now, which is either good news or ominous.

26

Miss Great Britain 2007

When I phoned Ashley to tell her about my experience with the journalist, she said that they had two places left for the Miss Great Britain competition and asked if I'd take part. I'd already decided I was never going to do that sort of thing again, but she was so nice and sounded so keen that before I knew it I'd agreed. As soon as I put the phone down, I thought, 'Oh my God, what have I done?' But then I suddenly realised there were so many other things going on in my life that I had no interest in winning, and it would be fun to take part without that pressure. Also, several girls from my agency were going to be contestants, and it would be a chance to support them and perhaps make more contacts for True Model Media.

So this time I was approaching the competition with a completely open mind and I really enjoyed it. All the girls were not only stunning, but also really nice and I made friends with loads of them. The pressure was off and it was so good not having to feel as though I was competing. I didn't have to try to prove anything, and it was an opportunity to try to correct the mistakes I'd made in the competition the previous year.

The only time I did 'lose it', very briefly, was when my mum said, 'Oh, Racheal, your hair's sticking up a bit at the back.'

I was immediately anxious and snapped at her, 'Why are you bothering about my hair? I don't care if my hair's sticking up. If you make me feel that I'm in competition with these girls, you'll crush me and I'll just want to go home.'

I can stand in a room among the most beautiful girls in the world and feel perfectly relaxed, but, no matter how much better I get, if I put myself in a situation of trying to compete, I just feel stupid. After all, it's even hard for the girls who *do* feel good about themselves. I knew I didn't deserve to win, but that didn't matter because it wasn't what I was there for; I was there to have a good time.

The trouble is that my mum's my mirror, and if she says something doesn't look OK, it can take my confidence away in a second. But she's too honest to lie to me and in fact I wouldn't really want her to, because at least I know she'll always tell me the truth.

When Mum realised she'd upset me she was contrite, but it had shaken my confidence and it only took one of the girls to ask me if I was OK to have me running off to hide in the toilets and cry until I'd got it out of my system. It was tiredness too, because I wasn't getting to bed before two in the morning and was waking up at about four, when Carly, my roommate, started getting ready. In fact, Carly was an angel and I couldn't have been put in a room with a better girl. She reminded me very strongly of Fay – with the same smile and hair – and we clicked immediately and found we were quite similar in lots of ways. So sharing with her really added to my enjoyment of the competition.

The competition took place on a Monday, and from the preceding Friday we stayed in a lovely five-star hotel with really good food. We all went to a chocolate and champagne party during the weekend, but most of the rest of the time it was extremely hard work. We were rehearsing for about 12 hours every day, just walking and walking, and with all that non-stop exercise I lost about five pounds – although I put it on again quite quickly after the weekend.

When I put on the dress they'd selected for me and came out of the changing room, Mum was just outside the door – which she shouldn't have been – and she looked at me and said, 'No.'

'What do you mean, "No"?' I asked her.

'I don't like it on you,' she replied. 'Tell them you're not wearing it.'

You're supposed to accept whichever dress you're given and be grateful, but, feeling really embarrassed, I went back into the changing room and said, 'My mum's bought me some beautiful jewellery and it's not going to match this dress. Can we change it?' Although the woman wasn't very pleased, she agreed, and I went out again in a bright-blue dress, and again Mum said, 'No!' I was mortified, because the woman was already a bit irritated and I knew I couldn't ask for another one.

Then Mum spotted a beautiful blonde girl who was wearing a dress she decided would be just right for me, and, ironically, just at that moment the girl approached me and asked if I'd be prepared to swap. As she was pale-skinned and blonde, the dress I'd been wearing looked stunning on her, and hers – a really beautiful dress by Jovani in lilacs and blues – looked much better with my colouring. So it worked out really well and we were both happy, and I hadn't had to undergo the humiliation of having to ask to change again.

There was a big 'shrine' to Danielle Lloyd at the competition in 2007, and Joan Rivers, who was the host, made some funny and typically caustic remarks about her. Also, because of what happened the previous year, the organisers had a chat with us beforehand, asking if anyone knew any of the judges and saying how unfortunate they thought it was that losing the crown had made Danielle more famous. I suppose it was because she was so unpopular as a result of what happened in the previous year's Miss Great Britain competition that the producers of *Big Brother* wanted her on the programme.

Even though I didn't look my best on the night of the competition, I had a really good time. I'd never had a chance to enjoy something like that before. In the first competition I entered, I was trying to overcome my fear, and the second time I had Danielle's unfriendly attitude towards me to contend with, which made me realise I wasn't as confident as I thought I was. But this time I was there to work, look after the girls from the agency who were taking part and enjoy myself, which is what I did. In fact, everyone who had taken part in the competition the previous year felt that the atmosphere among the girls was different this time.

Mum told me afterwards that she was really proud of me. 'I saw how hard you worked,' she said, 'and you didn't lose it once. You kept strong and sorted everything out.'

In fact, there was one particular incident that really showed me how far I'd come in only a couple of years.

The competition itself was held at the Grosvenor Hotel, and my brother and his wife were staying there over the weekend. So, just before the show started, I thought I'd go up to their room and wash my face and my fringe, which gets greasy by the end of the day. Although you're not really meant to leave the changing rooms, they were just beside the lift, so I thought it would be OK if I sneaked off quickly.

Wearing only my pyjamas and a pair of stilettos, and with no make-up on, I managed to get up to their room unseen and have a wash. But when I wanted to go back down again, I discovered you needed a special key to get to where I had to go. So there was no alternative but to go into the reception area, and as I was edging my way through it, feeling highly embarrassed, someone saw me and asked if I was OK. 'I'm just looking for the Miss Great Britain changing room,' I said, as nonchalantly as I could, but he obviously thought I was there to watch the final and said airily, 'Oh, just come through this way.'

Even though my pyjamas were black and quite respectable, I don't think I really fitted in with all the people arriving in ball gowns! But the next thing I knew I was face to face with all the celebrities having their pictures taken. Fortunately, the organiser, Robert de Keyser, saw me and pointed me in the right direction, and I had to run past all the paparazzi and the glamorous women in cocktail gowns in the bar area. It was like one of those terrible dreams when you're running around inappropriately dressed and in a panic and can't find your way back to where you're supposed to be – but it was actually happening.

As if all of that wasn't embarrassing enough, shortly after I got back to the safety of the changing room, someone came in and said, 'Could all the girls stay in here please, because the party's started outside and we can't have people running around in their pyjamas.'

When I thought about it afterwards, I felt quite proud of myself, because not all that long ago something like that would have caused me to have a panic attack, whereas this time I'd coped with it and could actually see the funny side.

What's interesting is that the girls at these competitions are completely different from what most people would expect, and a lot more insecure. I found that most of them understood me better than people I meet in day-to-day life, because they're used to being judged. A surprising number of them have been bullied and don't feel particularly good about themselves, and in a way they're looking for some kind of reassurance, which is sad, because they're such nice girls, and so pretty.

27

Living Life to the Full

As well as running True Model Media, I'm also being offered some exciting opportunities to do other things I really enjoy. For example, I was invited to be a judge for Miss London 2007 – an offer I accepted without being swayed at all by the fact that they were going to have a giant chocolate fountain. I have to admit that I do enjoy having the power to be able to judge the girls for what they're really like, rather than just in terms of their physical beauty. Obviously, there are certain criteria you look for – the way they speak and the way they carry themselves and so on – but there's also a need for them to have the right personality. It was also exciting because one of the prizes for the top three finalists in each of the regional heats was a year's contract with True Model Media.

For some reason, there seemed to be more bitchiness at Miss London than there is at the bigger competitions and I felt sorry for some of the contestants. When I turned up to do the judging, none of the girls knew who I was, and as I walked into the changing rooms to go to the toilet, smiling at anyone who looked at me, some of them didn't smile back and some gave me positively filthy looks. Later, when they came in for their pre-judging interviews, you could see them thinking, 'Oh ****, she's a judge!' A model friend of mine called Jessica was also working there and had the same experience, with some of the girls being very unfriendly – until they found out she worked for Model UK and suddenly all wanted to be her best friend.

Chico was a presenter as well as a performer at the competition and I ended up sitting at his family's table having a good old chat. They're really lovely people and very close as a family, and it was nice to see that Chico still has the same girlfriend. When he's performing he's just like he was on *X Factor*, but off stage he's a really sweet, laidback boy, not cheesy at all.

Chico's single, 'Coca Cola Body', is about size 0, and his brother, who's also his manager, talked to me about the possibility of working with me on my S.O.S. campaign. It was interesting to listen to a man's point of view about skinny girls and, because Chico's a very liked person, it would be good to have a role model like that who supports the campaign. So that's something quite exciting in the pipeline.

Another thing I've been involved with recently is helping a really sweet girl who was scouted from the Crawley area as a finalist in the next Miss England competition. I've been advising her, arranging her photo shoot and putting her in touch with all the people who sponsored me, and it's fun to see her enjoying doing all those things, which I rather missed out on.

I've also taken part in the filming of a documentary for the BBC, which is one of a series about body image called 'Am I Normal?'. The programme shows how I've got over my illness, and also incorporates True Model Media and the S.O.S. campaign to give people an idea of what I'm doing now.

As well as having to arrange a photo shoot with 12 of the models from the agency, all wearing S.O.S. T-shirts, I was interviewed by the series' psychologist, Dr Tanya Byron, who did *House of Tiny Tearaways* and who's really lovely. After she'd interviewed me, she suddenly said that she was going to take her make-up off on camera and asked if I'd be willing to do the same, to show how far I'd come. Initially, I was absolutely appalled because, although I feel comfortable being seen without my make-up by my family and by the people I'm used to, removing it on national television was quite a different matter. But then I thought about it and said, 'It's something I've never done, ever, for anything. But if this is what it takes to show people I can face my fear – and therefore so can they – then OK, I'll do it.'

So Tanya gave me a face wipe and I took off all my make-up on camera, and I was really proud of myself, because it was a huge step for me.

I know I'm going to hate watching the programme when it's shown on TV, but I have to remind myself that it isn't about what I look like. It's about showing people how far I've come and that it's really worth trying to overcome their own fears, because the things they're afraid of might turn out not to be quite so scary after all.

I realise it must seem to some people as though I'm someone who once had BDD and is now 'cured', or perhaps that I never really had the illness at all. But I think the reality is that it's an illness that never really goes away. I still wake up some days and feel I just can't face the world and long to pull the bedcovers over my head and hide. But, except on very rare occasions, I don't allow myself to take the easy way out. The more I pretended to be able to cope in the early days of my recovery, the more I found that the pretence was gradually slipping away and, to my surprise, I actually was coping. So, although I haven't been 'cured', and I know I never will be, I've learned to live with BDD and not allow it to control my life.

So the reason I take part in these programmes is because I want to show other BDD sufferers that if you can just force yourself to take those first steps towards facing your fears, you might find, like I did, that you've started on a journey of recovery. It won't always be easy – if ever – and you'll sometimes feel as though you're taking steps backwards, but it *is* possible.

Something else I've been involved in recently is a complete departure from anything I've done before. After I'd taken part in Miss Great Britain for the first time in 2006, I was contacted by someone from the limo company that sponsored a car to take me up to London for the final and asked if I'd like to enter the Miss Limo competition, which is done by voting. They allow you to add links to your profile on their website and I thought it would be a good way of promoting True Model Media, so I sent in some pictures. A few days later, they asked if they could change the pictures I'd chosen because, after looking at my website, they didn't think they did me justice – and suddenly I was top of the voting.

Then the organiser of the competition got in touch and asked if I'd like to compere the final. Although I hadn't presented anything before, I'm one of those people who'll take things on as a challenge, so I agreed. They put me up in a lovely suite in a hotel on a yacht the night before the competition, and as well as presenting the show, I had to interview all the girls on the phone, sort out the questions I was going to ask them and do all the choreography. It went really well and made me realise I much prefer being on that side of things rather than taking part in the competitions.

Another exciting thing I'm doing is hosting regular parties for an events company at some of the top clubs in the West End, such as Movida, Silver, Funky Buddha, Boujis, Punk and Cafe de Paris. All the models from True Model Media are invited, the girls and the guys, and it gives them a chance to do some networking with the organisers' guests – celebrities, people from the fashion industry, photographers and so on – while at the same time attracting people to the clubs. Sometimes the parties also include events such as competitions held by the photographer Mark Calligan, with a £1,000 portfolio as the prize. So it's fun for the models and gives me a chance to socialise with them all too.

I'm also doing more judging of competitions – and signing up the winners to True Model Media – including Miss Bikini Beach Babe and Hunk in Trunks at the Brighton Festival, which is held in aid of various charities.

A lot of the work I'm involved in now has come from contacts I made at Miss England and Miss Great Britain, so entering the competitions turned out to be a stepping stone towards being able to do the things I really enjoy.

But there is a downside to all the things I've been doing, which is that, even now, when I seem to be accepted by a lot of people and young girls come up to say hello and give me a hug when I go into Crawley, there are still people who wish me ill. For example, I had an email from someone quite recently, who I imagine is one of the people who used to bully me, saying they wish my mother and I would get breast cancer and die. I know it's stupid to be upset, and that the person who sent it obviously has serious problems of his or her own that are nothing to do with me, but you can't help being shocked by something like that. I don't understand why anyone would feel such ill will towards someone else, particularly someone they probably don't even know.

Then one day, not long after receiving that email, I found a large lump in my breast. I was really frightened because now I've learned to live with my illness and the modelling agency is going so well, the last thing I want to do is die. But I'm the sort of person who's quite funny about the idea of anyone examining me, and so, even though I was convinced it was cancer, I left it and left it until eventually it was so painful I had to pluck up the courage to go and see the doctor.

Part of the reason I was so sure it was cancer was because that somehow seemed to be what I might deserve. I'd taken life so much for granted and had tried to kill myself so many times that I felt dying now, when things were going so well, would be my punishment for wasting so much of my life. But, quite apart from the thought of dying, I was frightened by the prospect of having to have chemotherapy, and of what that would involve.

I didn't tell anyone when I found the lump, not even my mum, so I didn't have anyone to turn to and to discuss my anxieties with, and all I could do was look it up on the Internet. What I found was comforting in that a lump that's painful – which mine is – is less likely to be cancer, as cancerous lumps don't normally hurt. But I was still really worried.

Eventually, I told Paul about it, but we were going through a bad patch in our relationship at the time and he wouldn't even go to the doctor with me. So I had to go on my own and then wait for three very anxious weeks before it could be checked out.

Despite what I'd read on the Internet, I was still convinced it was cancer and became seriously depressed. Because of the problems Paul and I were having, I felt really alone and helpless, knowing that all I could do was sit back and take whatever happened. But I suppose the upside of all I've been through over the past few years is that I'm now really strong and nothing fazes me for long. Obviously, I do get low from time to time, but I've cried so much in my life that it takes a lot to reduce me to tears now – although I still cry whenever I think about Fay.

I found the examination mortifying and felt quite ill afterwards. They did a biopsy and took a sample from the lump and told me that it looked OK, but then I had to wait another few weeks for the test results and to have an ultrasound. It was a huge relief when the biopsy result came back negative for cancer, but still no one actually told me what it is. They just said that it's benign and 'nothing', but it's obviously 'something', because it's still there, seriously painful and getting bigger, and I'd like to know if anything can be done about it.

The trouble is that I'm too scared to put myself through that again, although I know I'm going to have to go back at some stage and get it sorted out. But I keep putting it off because I was so humiliated doing it the first time and the whole experience made me feel really uncomfortable. In fact, it was all made much worse by the surprising lack of sympathy and understanding shown by at least some of the staff at the hospital. For example, when I was being examined, the nurse said, 'Just take your top off,' which was horrible for someone who is even embarrassed when having to get changed in front of other girls. She could see I was trying to cover myself up, so she tossed a piece of tissue at me and said, 'You can cover yourself with that.' There didn't seem to be any understanding of how someone in those circumstances might be feeling, and the whole experience made me feel really dirty. I just wanted to get it done and get out, and was too embarrassed to ask any questions. But maybe you shouldn't have to ask questions in that sort of situation; maybe they should know how you're likely to be feeling and someone should sit you down and go through it all with you, rather than just saying, 'Oh, it's nothing,' and leaving you to it.

But, although it was a horrible experience, I'm really thankful it didn't have the outcome I was expecting, and I'm proud of myself for having been able to deal with it on my own.

28

Better the Devil
You Know ...

I'll always be grateful to Paul for all the help he gave me when I was so ill, and in some respects his tendency to ignore anything 'difficult' in the hope that it will go away was good for me, because it meant I tried to do things that no one else would have risked encouraging me to do.

I was about 17, and still very ill, when I went to Paul's house for the first time, and, because I was too shy and nervous to sit in the front room with all the family, I'd hide in the bedroom. But Paul's mum would knock on the door and say, 'What are you doing in there? Come downstairs.' It made me really frightened, but it happened each time we visited them, and she obviously thought I was just being rude. I can understand that it must have seemed like rather odd behaviour, but what she didn't seem to realise was that it was quite a significant achievement for me to make it round to their house at all.

If I did sit with Paul's family, they'd ask me questions – about the make-up I was wearing or about why I didn't get a job – which made me even more uncomfortable, because it felt as though I was being judged. There was a very hazy boundary between the disguise I wore and me, and it seemed they were criticising me personally, which made me want to try to avoid their interrogations. But, looking back, I can understand that they must have thought I was avoiding them and perhaps they took it personally.

Paul's sister is a very strong person and I know she found it hard to understand my behaviour, and, as sisters do, she was looking out for her brother. In fact, Paul would assure me I was the only girlfriend of his that his sister had ever liked, and she often used to send me beautiful Karen Millen clothes that she'd obviously only ever worn a handful of times. So she can't have hated me.

I think Paul's family just felt that asking me all those questions might make me think about what I was doing and change, and they didn't understand that, with an illness like BDD, that's not really possible.

Before the rest of Paul's family moved back to Scotland, we'd sometimes visit his grandparents there and would stay in a bed and breakfast next door to their house. Paul's mum couldn't understand why we didn't stay in his grandparents' spare room and would question us about it, which I found really upsetting, because again I realised they just thought I was being rude and didn't understand that I couldn't be seen without my make-up on. In fact, some days I couldn't leave our room in the B&B at all and we'd have to pretend I was ill. But Paul's grandparents were great; they'd seen me on *The Time, The Place* and so I think they understood me better than anyone else in his family.

In the early days of our relationship, Paul's mum didn't like me mentioning him when I did television and newspaper interviews. It seemed as though she was embarrassed and didn't want his name linked with mine, which was a bit hurtful because I was only saying how much he'd helped me. It's sometimes difficult to see things from other people's perspective, particularly when you have an illness like BDD, but I realise now that my behaviour must have seemed very strange to her at the time, and that any mother is bound to be more concerned for her own son than she is for someone outside the family.

Later, when the rest of Paul's family moved to Scotland, visiting them became even more difficult, because I'd be tired after the nine-hour drive and would just want to rest in the bedroom. But Paul's mum would follow me upstairs to ask what I was doing and to give me the day's itinerary. Eventually, I told Paul I couldn't bear it any more and said, 'Why don't you say something to your mum? Why does she follow me into the room? My mum wouldn't follow my brother's girlfriend everywhere she went, asking her what she was doing.' To which his rather bizarre reply was: 'She just likes being with you.'

However, on the last occasion I saw Paul's mum, she was talking to me in her usual way and Paul spoke up for me for the first time and said, 'Mum, stop bullying Racheal.'

His mum was obviously surprised and said, 'I had no idea,' which is when I realised it's just her way, and after that we finally understood each other.

I know his family must have thought I was being anti-social, and their 'pull yourself together' attitude in the early days of our relationship is one that's still shared by many people in relation to mental illness, particularly depression. But they've known me for nine years and, although I'm now different in many ways from the way I was when they first met me, I'm sure they realise I'm never going to be a completely 'normal' person. However, they do tell me how proud they are of how far I've come and often say that it's hard for them to believe how shy I used to be when I'm now such a chatterbox.

I'd had a chest infection just before we visited them in Scotland last time, and I was genuinely unwell, so I was upset when Paul was irritable with me. But then later I found out that while we were there, he'd been complaining about me in text messages he'd sent to a girl who hated me and who I was unaware he was friends with. I was very shocked and hurt, but eventually we talked about it and, although I was disappointed that he was saying negative things about me behind my back, I could understand his point of view. It must be difficult for him when people are always saying, 'Oh, poor Racheal,' and, 'You're so lucky to have someone like Racheal,' and he just wanted some of the attention to be focused on him. He wanted some praise for the way he's looked after me and for people to say, 'It must be difficult for Paul having to deal with Racheal.' I could sympathise with how he felt: BDD is a very 'selfish' illness as far as other people are concerned, because sufferers' attention is directed very much at themselves. But I just wished he'd spoken to me.

I always talk about Paul as though he's a knight in shining armour – which he has been, and I'll always love him because he helped me so much when I was ill. But I thought he was happy about the fact that I was so much better and able to do things with him, and it almost felt as though he wanted me to be ill and depressed again. As far as I know, he never did anything like that when I was ill. But he knows I need him most when I feel insecure, so perhaps there was a subconscious element to it – particularly as I was sure to find out about the text messages – in that he needed to be needed again, and the only way he knew of making me need him was to make me feel bad about myself.

I was speaking to another BDD sufferer recently who said her boyfriend treats her really badly but that she can't imagine being with anyone else, because when she has a BDD attack he's the only person who understands. Although Paul has never treated me badly, I do think our relationship is similar to some degree, because it seems that deep down inside himself he doesn't really like it when I'm happy and getting on with life and not so dependent on him.

Paul's the only boyfriend I've ever had – and he's also one of my best friends – and I feel comfortable and secure with him most of the time. He's done so much for me and has put up with so much from me. He doesn't try to control me or hold me, back from doing whatever I want to do, which is important to me, as I've been controlled by BDD nearly all my life and I don't think I could deal with that. I'd be scared to build a relationship with anyone else and, to be honest, I'm scared of the thought of seeing Paul move on with another girl, as it might make me take a step backwards. So, although I sometimes feel I'd like to whack him over the head, I do understand that he also has his own reasons for feeling insecure, and I don't blame him for any of it.

More recently, I discovered Paul had gone out with another girl behind my back – again someone I was bound to find out about. At one time, that would have been enough to make me try to kill myself, because I'd have thought there was something wrong with me – I'm not pretty enough, or my cooking's not good enough. But, although I was upset about it, I'm finally strong enough to be able to deal with it and to realise I'm not responsible for the things he does that hurt me. So, instead of sinking into depression and self-doubt, I booked myself a holiday abroad – having finally discovered that a change of scenery does me far more good than sitting around and moping.

Although I've come so far from the days when I was really ill, I know that, although I'm finally comfortable with who I am, the old insecurities will probably never leave me. I've been hurt by some of the things Paul has done recently, but we'll always be good friends and I'll always care about him. He's played such a large part in my life for so long that I don't feel as though I can ever lose him from it completely. Some people think he's bad for the things he's done that have hurt me, although, as far as I'm aware, none of it has been terrible, and it does seem as though he's wanted me to find out about it. But he's had to adapt to the fact that the girl he first met is now someone completely different, and perhaps he sometimes feels the need to say, 'Look! I'm here.'

In fact, the problems we've had really just illustrate some of the difficulties on both sides in any relationships involving BDD sufferers, who are probably less able than other people to deal with all the stresses. When they find someone who loves them for who they are and not for what they look like, they become reliant on that person and afraid to make a new relationship and run the risk of being rejected. It's quite difficult to explain to someone new how some days you can't be seen or to have to say, 'Don't look at me,' and, perhaps even more importantly, BDD sufferers don't like change.

29

Nature or Nurture?

No one really knows whether some people have a genetic tendency to develop BDD or whether it can occur in anyone under certain circumstances. From my own experience, I think it's a combination of nature and nurture, and that perhaps some people are born with a gene that predisposes them to BDD, but only some of them will develop the full-blown illness if they have particular experiences, which might be different for different people.

I realise now that my brothers used to have a bit of a tendency to obsess about their appearance, although obviously to a much lesser extent than I did, and their 'obsessions' were probably still within the 'normal' range. Looking back on it now, I think perhaps they suffer from a very minor degree of obsessive-compulsive disorder (OCD), which is apparently linked to BDD, and that we all share a personality trait in that we all want things to be a certain way.

For example, most people just do their hair and go; they don't keep doing it over and over again, and it doesn't have to be perfect. But I can remember, when I was about five or six and Jason was 17, he used to stand in front of the mirror, repeatedly flicking his hair for maybe an hour, and I'd stand beside him, mocking and mimicking him and joking around.

James also has similar tendencies. During the period when we went to Cyprus on holiday together, James had come home to live for a while and he would come into my bedroom before he went out and say, 'Racheal, I've got a rash on my forehead. Have you got anything to cover it up?' So I'd cover it up for him, but if he didn't think it was just right, he wouldn't go out. There was also one occasion when he wouldn't go out because he washed his hair about 20 times and still couldn't get it right.

Although that sort of thing didn't happen very often, the fact that it happened at all makes me wonder if we all have this tendency and it was exacerbated in my case by Fay's death and all the bullying.

When James was at school, he used to look up illnesses in Mum's medical book and then fake the symptoms, and he must have been pretty convincing, because the doctor would believe him too. I wonder now if that may have had more to do with getting signed off from school than with being a hypochondriac. But he was the most popular boy in school when I started at St Wilfrid's, and I was always coming across school desks with 'I love James Baughan' written all over them. It wasn't unusual for him to have 20 friends at the house at any one time, and quite a few of them ended up more or less living with us, until Dad bought a caravan for them to hang out in.

Parents don't know their children quite as well as their brothers and sisters do, and I think Mum just assumes that my brothers are all a little bit vain, but they're not. Geoff admitted to me once that he used to struggle even to approach a woman and that he never thought anyone was looking at him or was interested in him. In fact, all my brothers have always been very popular and they're all very good-looking, but they do have their insecurities, and I don't think they've ever really 'loved' themselves. I feel sad about that, because they should be full of confidence.

Obviously they don't have the same level of insecurities as I do, and even now I'm probably still worse than they are in that respect. One major difference between us is that they don't see themselves as disfigured or disabled, but they do have insecurities that stop them having the confidence in their looks that they should have. Ironically, although I think that makes them vulnerable to being taken advantage of by women, it probably also makes them good husbands, because they try to compensate for not feeling good about themselves by treating their women like princesses.

My dad has his problems too, and I think he suffers from a sort of 'social anxiety' in certain situations. For example, he didn't go with us to the Miss England competition because he thought people would look at him and think, 'How could someone who looks like that have produced that daughter?' He's really proud of me, and he seemed to think his presence at the competition would somehow detract from my moment in the limelight, which is really sad because *I'm* really proud of *him*.

The problem is that Dad doesn't feel attractive, and he sometimes gets really low about it. More than once in the past he's said to me, 'When I was growing up, Racheal, I always knew I was ugly. But I can live with that. I know what I am and I deal with it by making jokes about my looks. When I'm talking to someone, I look them straight in the eyes and make sure I hold eye contact with them so that their gaze doesn't drift to my face. But, when I look at my beautiful girl, I can't deal with it. You should be out there being happy.' Sometimes I just want to slap him and say, 'Stop it,' because he obviously doesn't see what I see when I look at him. But he won't allow anyone to reassure him, and there'd be no point anyway, because I know from my own experience that reassurance just goes in one ear and out the other.

I've spoken to Dad about the way he feels since I was diagnosed as having BDD, and we do see a connection, and I think it may have helped him to analyse himself and his own feelings a bit. But he won't agree that it's anything to do with our genes. He just thinks he's awful, when he's quite obviously not – which I think rather proves my point. Even people who aren't good-looking in the 'normal' way can appear so if they have an inner confidence, and Dad doesn't have that.

In fact, he's a very good-looking man, but if people say I look like him – and I do have very similar eyes – he won't have it, and says, 'No, no. She looks like her mother.' He doesn't want me to think I look like him because he feels that would be disappointing for me, and that, by comparing me with him, people are taking something away from me, and that's so not the truth. But he is rather contradictory, because, when I was going to Cambridge for the consultation about surgery, he said to me, 'If you have surgery, it would mean that you're ungrateful for the gift I gave you,' meaning my physical characteristics.

It may be that even before I was ill he used to make jokes about his appearance without me consciously noticing them. However, he wasn't around much when we were young, because he was always working, and I don't know whether my brothers and I would have picked up on how he felt when we were that age, and whether our tendency towards appearance concern is actually genetic or unconsciously learned.

Dad spends ages getting ready; he'll be in the bathroom for hours and hours if we're going out, and then sometimes, after all that, he won't go. But, on the other hand, he'll go to work dressed in the worst way he possibly can. He obviously doesn't want to try to make the effort to look nice because that would mean he'd be under pressure when people looked at him, which I think is very similar to me wearing jodhpurs when I was young: I didn't want to be seen to be *trying* to look pretty, because I knew I didn't. You'd just feel stupid if it was obvious to people you'd made terrific efforts to look nice and you still looked awful. But Dad doesn't go to quite the extremes I used to go to. He's a successful businessman and has obviously had to deal with these feelings all his life and has learned to cope with them. But the sad thing is that the way he deals with feeling unattractive – which he's not – is to make jokes about it, and it's very frustrating.

It's possible that the same tendency is in Mum a bit too. For example, she won't go to the door without make-up on, although in fact she looks beautiful without it, and ten years younger. I can remember her saying on several occasions, 'Someone's at the door. Quick, hide!' But in fact it isn't really an illness in Mum's case, because a lot of women don't like to be seen without their make-up on.

When I was ill I was always fussy about Mum not wearing anything too revealing. For example, I can remember one day when she was ready to go out and I started crying because I didn't want her to wear the outfit she had on. For Mum to be wearing a bodice was like her going out in her bra, and I felt really upset and disturbed, as though she was somehow being 'dirty'. I didn't mind what other people wore, but I had a real problem with it as far as Mum was concerned. But maybe that was something I picked up from my brothers, because if I ever wore a skirt that showed my knees, they'd say, 'No, don't go out in that. Wear this.' I suppose because I was already wearing loads of make-up, they didn't want me to dress older as well; being young men themselves, they were probably only too aware of the reactions I'd get.

So, nature or nurture? Apparently, it's possible that BDD occurs as the result of a combination of genetic and biological factors. Perhaps some people have genes for a personality type that tends to obsess and worry – which makes them more vulnerable to developing the illness – and also have a disturbance in their brain chemistry. If that's the case, it might help to explain why I see certain similarities between my own personality and the personalities of other members of my family, but, for whatever reason, my tendency to obsess and to want everything to be perfect is more pronounced.

Although it's still the case that relatively few people are aware of the existence of BDD, there is research being done into it, particularly in America, and there are treatments available that are apparently very effective for a lot of sufferers. The two main treatments are drug therapy with a type of drugs called serotonin-reuptake inhibitors (SRIs) and psychotherapy in the form of cognitive-behavioural therapy (CBT). The SRIs treat depression and obsessive thoughts and can reduce anxious behaviour such as mirror checking, while the CBT aims to modify certain beliefs and behaviours that cause emotional disturbance.

So, whatever the underlying cause, there is help available for people who suffer from BDD, and it's really important that they talk to someone who's aware that it's a specific – and treatable – illness.

30

Looking Back

When I started to do the television programmes, I think some people who felt they had some control over me saw how ill I looked and felt pleased about it. Perhaps it made them feel powerful to think that they'd put me there by making me feel bad about myself, and perhaps when I started to overcome the illness they felt they were losing their power over me. It's the only explanation I can think of for the really evil emails I occasionally received, which I think were from local people.

Although those emails were very upsetting, they did make me realise I'd done nothing wrong. If some people could still be nasty when I was doing things to try to help other BDD sufferers, it was obvious *they* had the problem rather than me. But I used to think it was my fault, because I hated who I was as well, so they were only validating my own opinion of myself. I think bullies can often pick up on someone's weakness – maybe the quiet child in the class, or the child who's poor and can't afford nice clothes, or the intelligent child who gets called a 'geek'. It's always something that makes them stand out in some way, something about them that's unique or special. But if you stand out because you're doing something you believe in – as I'm doing now – then you can deal with that.

It seems obvious that, for some people, bullying is the only opportunity they have to feel powerful and in control of something. For example, about two years ago, after I'd done Miss Great Britain, I was out one day, wearing a knee-length dress, and as I went past some guy he said, 'Oh, you should cover your legs up, love. You're too fat to wear that.'

I stopped and said to him, 'Did that make you feel cool in front of your friends? Could you please think twice about saying something like that to a woman. You've no idea what I've been through my whole life about my legs.'

He looked a bit uncomfortable and said, 'Well, actually I do know. That's why I said it. I know who you are and I thought it would get your attention.'

So it can only be a control thing, although it's a mystery to me why anyone would want the sort of attention a comment like that would get them.

That was the first time I'd ever had the confidence to respond to someone who made a nasty comment, and, although it was horrible and upsetting, it did make me realise how much stronger I'd become. There's no point trying to understand why people do things like that; what matters is that they'll never get me down again.

Until a few years ago, I still had abuse from some people in Crawley, I assume because they couldn't bear the fact that I was better and they no longer had a hold over me. But it doesn't happen any more. Now, when I go out into town, people come up and shake my hand and hug me, and what's really good is that there doesn't seem to be the bullying in the town that you used to see; the kids seem to have decided that it's not cool to be a bully. So, if the publicity I've had locally about my illness has had some impact in that respect, that's really worthwhile and I'm very pleased.

Looking back over my life to write this book, I began to see connections I'd never previously realised were there. Some of them seem glaringly obvious now, and I wonder how I never saw them before. But, unless you make a deliberate attempt to examine and analyse all the apparently disjointed events of your life, you don't see the bigger picture, just the corner of it that you're inhabiting at the time.

I think now that my appearance concerns probably started at a younger age than I've always thought – possibly at about 10 or 11, when I began to carry around the Dermablend concealer. Although I used to pretend I didn't care about what I looked like, the truth is that I'd already realised I wasn't pretty and I secretly desperately wanted to be, despite the fact that it went against everything I thought I believed in. What helped me deal with it to a certain extent was the fact that I saw myself as a tomboy, so I just went with the 'horsey girl' image and didn't even try to be anything else. But it's obvious to me now that I *was* concerned about what people thought about my looks and was desperate to look acceptable without appearing to have tried. Then, when people started to bully me, I could no longer ignore the fact that I just didn't fit in.

I think in my case the bullying started because my family were quite wealthy and I was very shy and just wanted to fit in and have some friends. It made me an easy target to extract money from, because I was so desperate to be liked that I'd give away my school dinner money and just not eat.

Although I never used to look at the 'popular' crowd and wish I were one of them, I did want to be accepted, but I always felt I looked different. From the moment I started school, the other kids made comments about my eyes, and I had a complex about them for years. I have blue eyes and I always wanted brown, and

I'd ask my parents if I could have brown contact lenses. Then, when I was a bit older, people used to say I looked stoned and call me a 'druggie' – either that or a 'Paki'. Although it ruined my life for several years and has still left me vulnerable in some respects, it also made me strong; I can take almost anything now.

It's very upsetting for Mum when she reads some of the things people have said about me, but I've reached a stage when I can only be hurt by the opinion of someone I care about. Also, I realise they only say those things because they're insecure. That doesn't mean I don't still have my own insecurities, but they're different, and I would never say horrible things about other people. Jealousy – whether it's about someone else's wealth, intelligence, beauty or whatever – is a really nasty thing, and it must be very sad to live your life feeling bitter and needing to judge other people. I'd spent so many years being terrified that people were going to judge me that I think that's partly why I did Miss England: I just thought, 'Go on then. Judge me all you like. I really don't care.'

What I want to do is talk about BDD and what it involves in the hope that increased awareness of the illness will enable people who suffer from it to get the help they need. Knowing about my experiences might make someone say, 'She was able to do that, so perhaps I can too.'

I still get a certain amount of personal criticism, perhaps because people realise they can get at me that way, and some people say, 'Oh, you didn't have BDD in the first place,' which is really hurtful when I've fought so hard to overcome it. But all I can do is put something out there and let people take from it what they want. I can't control their reactions. I can only try my best to make people with BDD who are open to the idea aware that there *is* help available for them and that it *is* possible to get better. It may be a long and slow process, and there may be many setbacks along the way, but then that's true of most things that are really worth doing. You just have to set yourself small goals that will eventually enable you to reach the bigger goal you're aiming for. Sometimes you'll fail, but that's all right. When you're trying to do something as difficult as overcome a serious illness like BDD, there are bound to be times when you don't immediately succeed, and you're allowed to be disappointed. But then you have to pick yourself up and try again, or adjust that particular goal to something more realistically achievable – and one day you'll look back as I do now and be proud of how far you've come.

Naturally there are still days when I wake up and feel low, particularly when I've been very busy and am starting to feel tired. But now I'm able to force myself to get up and out of the house to do whatever I have to do, and I know I'll be fine – and that's the difference. When I was ill, if I did manage to force myself out of the house, I'd regret it and it wasn't ever fine, whereas now it's just that first step that's sometimes hard to take, and then I'm OK. And that's an important thing for anyone with BDD to understand. There's no point someone telling you that if you push yourself to do something you'll be fine, because that's simply not true; you're not going to feel better instantly. The first time you attempt to do something that goes against your inclination to hide yourself away, you're probably going to end up feeling defeated and awful. But, over a period of time, things gradually start to fall into place. So it's important to be realistic and not to think that every day will be a good one.

For me, the major turning point was doing Miss England and discovering that, although I was really frightened, I ended up feeling proud of myself and realising I'd taken a huge step forward. However difficult I might find it, I now try my best to take advantage of anything that's offered to me, and I don't turn down opportunities because of my illness.

Looking back over my life while writing this book has helped put things in perspective. Recently, when I was a bit low again after finding out about the text messages Paul had been sending about me, I think Mum was anxious that I might be about to go downhill. I'd gone to see my doctor because I had a chest infection I just couldn't get rid of, and as I opened the door to the surgery, he asked if I was OK, as he always does, having witnessed the roller-coaster of my illness over the past few years. But this time I burst into tears and said, 'No, I'm not. I feel as though I'm always having to make out to the world that I'm OK because there are people relying on me. But I don't feel OK any more.'

The doctor gave me some anti-depressants, but, having read on the packet that one of their side effects can be suicidal thoughts, I decided not to take them, as it didn't seem a very good idea for someone who used to feel like killing herself anyway. But, even without any medication, the depression passed, and I realised it's normal to have periods when things get on top of you. Who doesn't have times when they feel worn out and under pressure and when they long to stop putting on a brave face and just hide away? What it's important to remember is that some days won't be as good as others, but you can still deal with them. Anyone would be very fortunate to wake up every day and think, 'Oh, I look beautiful!' So having a bad day is just a normal part of being human.

When you've been ill and have felt despair and hopelessness, you have to keep reminding yourself that it's all right for anyone, however positive and happy their lives normally are, to feel despondent and miserable occasionally, and to have days when they're sick of making the effort.

Sometimes things happen that shock me and then I'm reminded of how I used to feel, but I know now that I'm in control of the bad days and that I won't allow BDD to take control of my life again. I was ill for about seven years and, although I may never be completely better, I'm not ill now. I may always be more anxious than other people and more prone to insecurities, but now when I start to feel low I recognise it and I know I can fix it by doing something positive. I just need to remind myself from time to time that the real me is the person inside, and that that person isn't a bad person.

There will always be two of us – me and the girl with BDD – but I've left that girl behind in the past and that's where I want her to stay. She comes back to haunt me from time to time, and even to this day I can't curl my hair or wear a lipstick colour I used to wear because it takes me back to when I was so ill. But I know she won't stay around for long.

I may never feel good about myself, but that doesn't matter. My life isn't focused on what I look like any more because I realise that's superficial. My body is just a shell that won't last for ever anyway; it's *who* you are that really matters.

People laugh at me when I say I'm shy, as I really don't come across as a shy person. But it's the truth. It's just that I've learned how to deal with it – partly by talking a lot. I'm almost the opposite of what I used to be in that respect: I could stand up today in front of 1,000 people and give a speech, whereas I'd have struggled to talk to just one person a few years ago. I use the technique I call 'Lights! Camera! Action!' every day: whatever I'm doing, I tell myself I'm Cindy Crawford and then I'm fine!

My brothers used to get really upset when they saw me screaming and having panic attacks, and they'd try to make Mum leave me alone. But, although I hated her at the time and was really angry with her, I realise now that she was right. If she hadn't forced me to face my fear, I might still be shut away in my bedroom today, miserable and defeated and with the prospect of a life that wasn't worth living – or worse. I've spoken to other sufferers who say they take things out on their mums and dads too, and I try to reassure them that it's not their parents who are to blame. The irony was that, despite being angry with her, my mum was always the person I wanted with me. On the rare occasions when I did try to go into town, she had to be there at my side; but of course, if I had a panic attack while we were out, I always blamed her.

It must have been terrible for Mum. She didn't know how to help me or where to find anyone else who would understand how seriously ill I really was, and she must have felt some of the despair and frustration I was feeling. She was so desperate to get me out of my room and to make me happy that she'd offer to buy me anything I wanted. My friends would come round and say, 'Come on, Racheal, please. Your mum's going to take us all shopping,' but I'd just say, 'No. No, I'm sorry. I can't.' So sometimes they'd end up going shopping with Mum for the things I needed, while I stayed at home.

Now I can look back with pride on all those television programmes and interviews Mum made me do, in the knowledge that overcoming my dread of being seen and speaking out about my illness may have helped raise people's awareness of BDD and given comfort to other sufferers.

I was talking to a friend the other day, a really lovely boy who I hadn't realised had become quite depressed, and he was telling me how he turns on people when he's feeling bad and can be really nasty to them, and then feels awful because he doesn't mean to do it. I didn't recognise the person he was describing, but I could completely understand what he was saying, and it hit home to me that that was exactly how I used to feel. I used to get angry with people and take it out on them rather than admit I had a problem, which simply reinforced my feeling that I wasn't a nice person. But I know now that I reacted that way because the illness was in control – and it's the same for anyone with BDD, depression, anxiety or any similar psychological problem.

I'm now able to separate myself from the illness and see that this is me, and this is the illness. So I don't hate the person I was, but I do hate BDD and what it was making me become, and I'm determined not to let it take control of my life again. I believe now that I was never actually the person it made me feel I was, because I know how much guilt and anger I felt on the inside. But it *was* controlling me, and I'd wake up and think, 'Oh my God, I've been so nasty to everyone, I'm just going to have to kill myself,' and I'd punch myself or hurt myself in some way because I hated who I was.

I know I'm never going to see myself as looking good, but I don't care any more. My mum still has to choose my photos, because they all look dreadful to me, but I've learned to accept that it doesn't matter what I look like. What's important is being able to face the world and do all the things I want to do without BDD holding me back. Now I do day-to-day things to contradict what the illness is telling me. For example, if it tells me I can't do something, I'll do it. So, although BDD may never go away completely, I now know how to fight it – and I do fight it every single day of my life.

When I was ill, everything was relatively all right *before* I tried to get ready and put all my make-up on. It was attempting to face the world that led to the BDD attacks, because it was just so hard trying to paint a perfect portrait on my face. The sadness for me at that time was in desperately wanting to do something and knowing I couldn't. I'd want to get ready so I could go out with my friends, or just be able to eat a normal meal with my family, but that meant having to look in the mirror to paint on my mask and try to fix what was wrong. Sometimes I could be relatively content alone in my room, hidden away like the Phantom of the Opera, but the disappointment and frustration I felt when I failed to create the perfect disguise would push me back into a downward spiral of self-loathing and anger.

I think we're all here for a reason, and maybe I was meant to go through all those miserable years so that I could help other people. I'm certainly a strong person now, and I like the Racheal who's come out on the other side of the illness. I'm also fully aware that, if I hadn't gone through it, I could have been quite a different person, and probably someone I'd be considerably less proud of. So, in a way, something good did come out of it all.

I know that to some people the symptoms of BDD seem like vanity, so one thing that really does need emphasising is how serious and disabling an illness it really is, and how much misery and heartache it can bring, not only to sufferers themselves, but also to their families and friends. People sometimes say – or at least would like to say – to BDD sufferers, 'Oh, come on. There's nothing really wrong with you. Just think of the people who have to live each day of their lives in wheelchairs. At least you've got all your limbs,' and I can understand how frustrated they must feel. But they don't know what it's like; it feels as though you *are* living in a wheelchair or have some other severe physical disability that prevents you being able to do the things you want to do. The truth is that BDD is a psychological disability that's as debilitating as any physical illness.

When I was ill, I hated my legs, and one day about eight years ago, after I'd been on television, a journalist phoned from a newspaper and said, 'There are two men with BDD who've just had their legs amputated. How do you feel about that?'

Although I wasn't as ill as I had been, I could remember clearly how I'd felt, and so I said, 'Well, if I could have had my legs amputated, I would have. So I can completely understand how they felt.' The journalist was absolutely shocked, and I tried to explain. 'I'm sorry,' I told her. 'I'm not saying it's right; I'm just saying that I *can* understand how they felt. But I do think it's disgusting that the surgeon agreed to do it.' It was scary, because I'm sure I would have wanted to have my legs amputated if it had been possible, so I do feel it should never have been allowed to happen.

Later, I read the surgeon's explanation of why he'd agreed to do it. It appears that the two men had a specific, and relatively rare, type of BDD that had made them convinced since childhood that they would only ever be happy if they had one of their, perfectly healthy, legs removed. So the surgeon, feeling they were already severely disabled by the misery of their lives, had finally done the operations. I don't think such a thing would be allowed today, and I think there was a lot of trouble about it at the time, but it does go to show how important it is that more people are made aware of BDD as an illness and of the fact that there are successful non-surgical treatments available for it.

Of course, everyone's experience of BDD is different, but one thing I think all sufferers probably have in common is that they're unlikely ever to get to the point when they're happy with what they look like. The key is to get past that and learn to live a normal life.

Obviously I'm not saying that everyone should do what I've done and enter Miss England or Miss Great Britain – they're just silly, meaningless things really, which I've done to face my own particular fear. But what I *am* saying is that suffering from BDD can stop you doing anything at all, and can make you miss out on so much. So what you have to learn to do is take all the opportunities that come your way, and not allow the illness to keep you suspended at arm's length from life – and I hope this book will show people that it is possible to reach that point.

I know that if I allowed myself to start getting the mirror out, I might run the risk of going backwards, and I can't let myself do that. So I have to be constantly aware of that possibility and fight the urge whenever it arises. I've been very lucky in that I have the added incentive of knowing that some people look to me for hope and I can't let them down, although at times that can feel like a heavy responsibility. Of course, I still have bad days now and again, when I get really low and wish I wasn't here. But I can't allow myself to succumb to depression and inertia, because that would mean taking away from all those people the hope of being able to get better, and it's that thought that keeps me going and helps prevent me ever getting as low as I used to be.

Perhaps BDD affects people who have low self-esteem and a tendency to be over-anxious perfectionists, and perhaps you never really completely get over the illness. But I think what my own experience illustrates is that, with help, you *can* learn to live with BDD and to manage it so that it doesn't control and destroy your life. The help I needed came from several sources, primarily from my mum's determination not to give up on me and from going on the TV programmes and starting to understand I had an illness and wasn't just a 'bad person'. The TV shows gave me the opportunity to communicate with other people who were going through the same experiences, and that made me realise I wasn't alone and that I could do some good by trying to help other BDD sufferers.

Comparing the letters people sent me with their photographs made me start to accept the fact that BDD is an illness based on an illusion, a misperception of what you're seeing when you look in the mirror. But that understanding is just the first step towards learning to live with it. I know it's very difficult for many people to see BDD as anything other than excessive vanity. But what I've learned over the last few years is that it's a serious and debilitating illness that distorts the self-image of sufferers and makes their lives a misery.

'Getting better' doesn't mean you're able to look in the mirror and see what other people see when they look at you. The image reflected back at me today is the same as the image I've always seen, but at least now I have a little voice in my head telling me it's an illusion. Sometimes the voice is so quiet that I have to struggle to hear it, but more often these days it's loud enough to remind me that I need to walk away from the mirror and get on with my life.

Looking Back

Over the last few years, I've had to reassess everything I thought I knew about myself and try to discover what sort of person I really am. It hasn't been an easy journey, and it's one I know I'll be travelling for the rest of my life. But I've come a long way and I'm not about to give up now.

I feel so alone and maybe I deserve it!

WHY?

What the fuck is wrong with me?

Why do I feel like every day is pain life is nothing but a punishment I hate it. I am so obsessed by my looks that I can not even leave the house anymore. every one hates me even people I get close to get driven away by my obsession I am so depressed no one understands me they all think I am stupid that I have nothing to worry about but they are not the ones who have to live in this body I need help I wish so much that I could die I have no energy or motivation to do anything to sort my life out I feel so weak and ill I am always crying I know that the only reason I have friends is because they feel sorry for me and dont think I could live without them and they are right I couldn't. ok so I have got my family but even they must see me as nothing but a burdon and I have a boyfriend but how long will that last? I mean I could never go out with someone like me and still I know that he is sick of me but does not know how to tell me. So really I dont think that their is anyone who really actively likes me for me I am sure that they all would want me to change and I really want to change but I am Trapped with this mind this fucked up weird twisted mind I hate me so much everything even my personality what do I contribute to this world nothing and I know that it is not long before I loose everything my friends my boyfriend and my family will dissepear one by one and then I will be alone left in pain to die slowley of lonlyness and deppression.

A letter I had written to myself during a BDD attack.

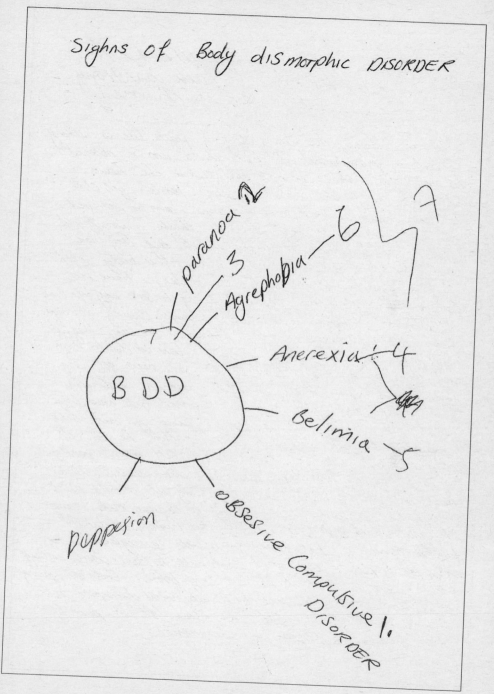

A chart of symptoms I drew while I was trying to understand BDD.

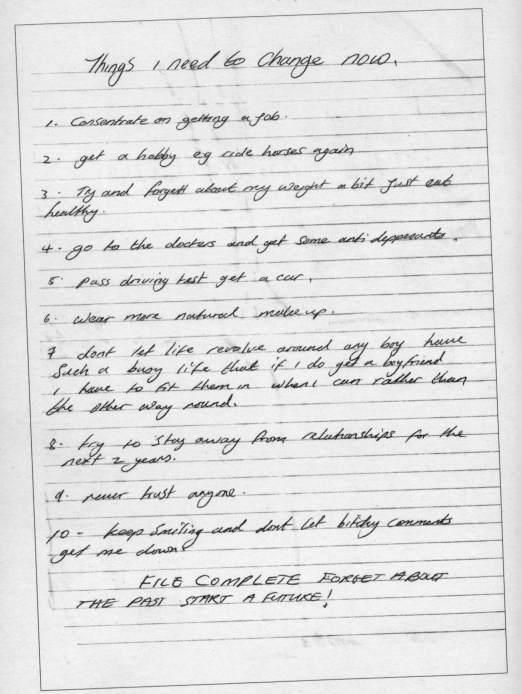

Things i need to change now.

1. Consentrate on getting a Job.

2. get a hobby eg ride horses again

3. Try and forgett about my weight a bit Just eat healthy.

4. go to the doctors and get some anti deppesants.

5. pass driving test get a car.

6. wear more natural make up.

7 dont let life revolve around any boy have Such a busy life that if i do get a boyfriend i have to fit them in where i can rather than the other way round.

8. try to stay away from relationships for the next 2 years.

9. never trust anyone.

10 - keep smiling and dont let bitchy comments get me down

FILE COMPLETE FORGET ABOUT THE PAST START A FUTURE!

I wrote a list of goals I wanted to achieve.

The Samaritans

The website for the Samaritans is www.samaritans.org. Their phones are manned 24 hours a day, every day of the year. The number in the UK is 08457 90 90 90 (charged at the cost of a local call) and in the Republic of Ireland it's 1850 60 90 90. The organisation is also a member of Befrienders Worldwide, which provides a similar service in 40 countries around the world (www.befrienders.org).